VOL. 59

COVERS ALL STRAIGHT WING
F-84 THUNDERJET VERSIONS.

F-84 THUNDERJET

in detail

A DETAIL & SCALE AVIATION PUBLICATION

Bert Kinzey

squadron/signal publications

COPYRIGHT © 1999 BY DETAIL & SCALE, INC.

This book is a product of Detail & Scale, Inc., which has sole responsibility for its content and layout, except that all contributors are responsible for the security clearance and copyright release of all materials submitted. Published by Squadron/Signal Publications, 1115 Crowley Drive, Carrollton, Texas 75011.

CONTRIBUTORS AND SOURCES:

David Menard
Lloyd Jones
Bill Paul
Jim Galloway

Stan Parker
Jim Roeder
The United States Air Force Museum, Dayton, Ohio
The Museum of Aviation, Warner Robins, Georgia
The 166th Tactical Fighter Squadron of the Ohio Air National Guard, Springfield, Ohio

Detail & Scale and the author express a sincere word of thanks to David Menard for his generosity in loaning several dozen original color slides for use in this publication.

A special word of thanks is also expressed to the United States Air Force Museum. The museum's Research Division was absolutely essential during the research and preparation of this publication. Numerous detailed photographs of the museum's excellent F-84E also appear on the following pages.

The author is also very grateful to Bill Paul of the Museum of Aviation at Warner Robins, Georgia. Bill patiently assisted the author on three different trips to the Museum of Aviation to photograph the F-84E on display there.

The 166th Tactical Fighter Squadron of the Ohio Air National Guard deserves another special word of thanks. Personnel of the unit were particularly helpful in assisting the author in taking photographs of the refueling receptacle on the F-84G which is on display at the Springfield Air National Guard Base.

Many photographs in this publication are credited to their contributors. Photographs with no credit indicated were taken by the author.

ISBN 1-888974-12-5

Above (front cover photo): "LIL BUTCH" was F-84E-25-RE, 51-478, and it was assigned to the 9th Fighter Bomber Squadron of the 49th Fighter Bomber Wing in Korea. It stands on the perforated steel plating (also known as Marston matting) ready for its next mission against the communists, and it is armed with two 500-pound bombs and four 5-inch rockets. JATO units are attached to the underside of its aft fuselage.

(Galbraith via Menard)

Right (rear cover photo): Cockpit details and colors in the F-84E on display at the United States Air Force Museum at Dayton, Ohio, are illustrated in this large photograph. For additional pictures taken in the cockpit of this Thunderjet, see pages 42 and 43.

INTRODUCTION

Heavily armed with rockets, this F-84E exemplifies the fighter-bomber role at which the Thunderjet excelled during the Korean War. Although many publicity photographs like this one show rockets stacked in threes or even fours under the wings, the manuals indicate that rockets were only to be loaded in singles or stacked in pairs for operational use. Twelve-inch Tiny Tim rockets are loaded on the two pylons. (USAFM)

The common perception of a fighter aircraft is that of a sleek swift mount flown by a dashing pilot who has excelled in aerial combat and become an ace. History books, novels, documentaries, and Hollywood's movies have all glamorized the fighter aces and the airplanes they flew. Like the men who flew them, fighter aircraft have also been judged primarily on their success in air-to-air combat.

While it is not surprising that the aces and the fighters they flew receive the major share of recognition and glory, an objective study of military aviation history will reveal that less than one percent of all fighter pilots have ever achieved the coveted status of ace by shooting down five or more enemy aircraft. From World War I to Operation Desert Storm, far more fighter sorties have been flown to attack targets on the ground than to engage enemy aircraft. In every war, these mundane and almost unnoticed missions have been every bit as important as aerial combat in determining the final outcome of armed conflict. Confronted by everything from small arms fire to sophisticated guided missiles, the pilots who flew these missions faced great danger, and many more fighters have been shot down by ground fire than by an enemy aircraft.

Fighters that spent most of their operational service attacking targets on the ground have been almost forgotten by history in spite of the significant contributions they made. Republic's F-84 Thunderjet is a primary example of such a fighter that has never received the recognition it deserves.

Designed during World War II, the Thunderjet was among America's first generation of jet fighters. Along with its contemporaries, such as the F-80 Shooting Star and the Navy's F9F Panther and F2H Banshee, it had simple designs with straight wings that prevented the full increase in performance that jet engines promised. Likewise, the first turbojet powerplants were not fuel efficient, and their non-afterburning designs provided rather anemic thrust.

By the time the Korean War began in 1950, these first generation jet fighters were inadequate for air-to-air combat when compared to the swept wing designs like the F-86 Sabre and the Russian MiG-15. But Korea was a war fought far more on the ground than in the aerial arena of MiG Alley. Thousands of sorties were flown by these first generation fighter-bombers against important targets in North Korea, while even more provided United Nations forces on the ground with critical close air support. Of these, 86,408 sorties were flown by F-84 Thunderjets. While the books and movies about the air war in Korea may concentrate almost exclusively on the air-to-air combat between the F-86 Sabre and the MiG-15, the contributions of the F-84 Thunderjet were even more significant. Throughout the conflict, it proved to be the most effective and successful fighter-bomber in the Air Force's inventory.

But the contributions of the Thunderjet go well beyond what it accomplished in Korea. The F-84G was the first production fighter-bomber to be fitted with an inflight refueling capability, and it was the first fighter-bomber to have the ability to deliver an atomic weapon. Both of these firsts were extremely important in the development of military aviation and they led to the significant capabilities that today's fighters have.

This publication covers each version of the F-84 Thunderjet, and it provides a detailed look at the F-84E and F-84G which were the most numerous and important variants. Photographs and drawings illustrate every feature of the aircraft, and most of the detailed photos were taken specifically for this publication. Aviation historian, author, and artist, Lloyd Jones, has created 1/72nd scale drawings exclusively for this book that illustrate the important changes made from one version to the next. A modeling summary covers all of the plastic scale model kits of the F-84 Thunderjet and recommends the best ones in each scale.

HISTORICAL SUMMARY

The very simple lines of the Thunderjet are illustrated in this view of the first XP-84-RE experimental prototype. The aircraft was painted overall gloss gray with black markings. **(USAFM)**

During World War II, most aircraft manufacturers were busy producing several types of aircraft for the Army Air Force, the Navy, or even both services in some cases. But at Republic, almost the entire effort was dedicated to the production of the P-47 Thunderbolt. Although this excellent design would establish an outstanding record in combat, and it would be produced in greater numbers than any other U. S. fighter aircraft in history, the curtain was coming down on the Thunderbolt's service and production even before the war ended. In Europe, General "Jimmy" Doolittle had openly expressed a preference for the North American P-51 Mustang, and within the Eighth Air Force, only the 56th Fighter Group remained operational in Thunderbolts when Germany surrendered.

The long range P-47N variant was being delivered to the Pacific theater where missions lasting as long as nine hours were being flown over the Japanese mainland from the island of Ie Shima. But production orders were declining, and the Republic's management knew that their financial survival depended on developing a new aircraft that could be produced in the lean years following the end of the war with Japan.

It was with both concern and enthusiasm that Republic considered the General Operational Requirements (GOR) issued by the Army Air Force on September 11, 1944. This GOR called for the development of a midwing day fighter having a top speed of 600 miles-per-hour and a combat radius of 850 miles. Initially, the requirements also specified an internal armament consisting of eight .50-caliber machine guns or six .60-caliber weapons, but this was later changed to six .50-caliber guns in order to save weight. The radius of action requirement was also reduced to 705 miles. The Army Air

Force also stipulated that the aircraft would be powered by the General Electric TG-180 axial-flow gas turbine engine which was being developed under the direction of the Air Technical Service Command. Production of the engine would subsequently be turned over to the Allison Division of General Motors.

With the development of jet engines still in its infancy, the Army Air Force wanted to explore as many different variations as possible to insure that at least one design was successful. As a result, the Bell P-59 Airacomet used the axial-flow J31 powerplant developed by General Electric. The TG-180 was a further development of the axial-flow design that would soon be redesignated the J35. By comparison, Lockheed's P-80 Shooting Star was powered by the centrifugal-flow J33, and North American's F-86 was fitted with the J47 which was another axial-flow design.

Although the engineers at Republic originally contemplated redesigning the P-47's airframe to meet the specifications stated in the GOR, it quickly became apparent that the Thunderbolt's large bulbous fuselage could not be streamlined sufficiently to accept a jet engine. As a result, an entirely new design proposal was offered by Republic in early November 1944. It was quite simple and featured straight wings with conventional control surfaces. The design of the axial-flow engine permitted a very slender aft fuselage, and Republic opted for a single air inlet in the nose rather than using two which were buried in the wing roots as Lockheed had done on their P-80. As a result, the fuselage was much more streamlined than that of the Shooting Star, and therefore it produced less drag. The pilot's cockpit was covered by a simple strong windscreen and a sliding bubble canopy that provided excellent visibility. Internal armament was to be four .50-caliber machine guns mounted in the nose.

On November 11, the Army Air Force authorized Republic to proceed with the development of a mockup, a static test article, and three prototypes. Less than two months later, on January 4, 1945, a letter contract was issued for twenty-five service test aircraft and seventy-

The three XP-84 experimental prototypes were followed by fifteen YP-84A test and evaluation aircraft. Serial number 45-59485 was the third YP-84 built, and its full designation was YP-84-2-RE. Unlike the three XP-84s, the YP-84s were unpainted natural metal. **(USAFM)**

five production aircraft. This was later changed to fifteen service test aircraft, which were designated YP-84As and eighty-five production examples designated P-84Bs. The three prototypes, already under development, received the XP-84 designation.

Work proceeded at a rapid pace, and the mockup inspection was conducted in early February 1945. Although judged to be generally satisfactory, several design changes were ordered to be incorporated into the prototypes.

By the end of 1945, the first airframe was ready, and it was rolled out in December. However, the J35 engines were not yet available, and the initial flight was delayed until February 28, 1946. In the interim, the aircraft had been disassembled and flown to Muroc Flight Test Base in California, which is today's Edwards Air Force Base.

In late 1946, the name "Thunderjet" was bestowed on the aircraft as a way of keeping alive the heritage begun with Republic's famous P-47 Thunderbolt. This "Thunder" name would be continued on later Republic fighter aircraft in the form of the F-84F Thunderstreak, RF-84F Thunderflash, and F-105 Thunderchief, all of which served the U. S. Air Force in the tradition first established by the Thunderbolt during World War II.

As expected, early flight testing revealed that overall performance was indeed superior to that of Lockheed's P-80 Shooting Star, but some problems were also encountered. The skin on the tail section buckled and wrinkled, and longitudinal instability was discovered in wind tunnel tests. The weight of the aircraft was also too high, and ways had to be found to reduce it to acceptable levels.

Delays in the delivery of the J35 engines complicated matters, and the second XP-84 did not fly until the following August. By the time the third prototype was finally delivered, some of the problems had been solved, and the engine had been changed to the J35-A-15 which offered 4,000 pounds of thrust. This was 250 pounds more than the J35-GE-7 installed in the first two prototypes. As a result of these improvements, the third prototype was redesignated XP-84A.

By February 1947, the fifteen YP-84As were joining the three prototypes in the flight test program, and the first P-84B production aircraft were starting to roll down the assembly lines. To meet the specifications of the GOR, internal armament had been increased to six .50-caliber machine guns, with two being located in the wing roots in addition to the four in the nose.

The first production version of the Thunderjet was the P-84B, eighty-five of which were ordered with the fifteen YP-84As. To this number, another 141 were added bringing the total produced to 226. Deliveries began in June 1947, and the first unit to receive the P-84B was the 14th Fighter Group at Dow Field near Bangor, Maine. The group reached its Initial Operational Capability (IOC) in December 1947, but numerous problems plagued the program for quite some time. Many of these had to do with the fact that aircraft engineers were still in a steep learning curve as they tried to figure out the best way to design jet aircraft. They were faced with the challenge of meeting performance specifications while insuring that the airframe remained structurally sound. At the same time, the aircraft and all of its systems had to be easy to maintain as well.

Access for maintenance on the P-84B was far from satisfactory, and it earned a reputation of being a "mechanic's nightmare." This was complicated by a lack of trained ground personnel that were competent to work on the new jets. Critical shortages of spare parts made the situation even worse, and as a result, the operational readiness of the squadrons fell below acceptable levels.

There were severe structural problems with the air-

The first production version of the Thunderjet was the F-84B, and the first operational unit was the 14th Fighter Group at Dow Air Force Base, Maine. This F-84B was assigned to the 49th Fighter Squadron which was part of the 14th Fighter Group. (USAFM)

craft as well. Restrictions had to be placed on speed and G-loads, and in May 1948 the entire fleet was grounded for inspection. Modifications had to be made to each aircraft at considerable cost before they were safe to fly again without any restrictions.

On September 18, 1947, the U. S. Army Air Force became the U. S. Air Force as a separate branch of America's armed services. On June 11, 1948, it did

away with the old pursuit designation (P-) and replaced it with fighter (F-). The P-84 thus became the F-84 on that date, and the prefix for buzz numbers used on Thunderjets had to be changed from **PS** to **FS**. By that time, F-84Cs were rolling off the assembly lines at Farmingdale, but these aircraft differed little from the F-84B. They experienced the same structural problems and had to receive the strengthening modifications required by the F-84Bs. All 191 F-84Cs had been delivered to the U. S. Air Force by November 1948.

Named "MISS MINUCKI," this F-84B-30-RE was used as an instructional airframe at Chanute AFB, Illinois. (USAFM)

General ARRANGEMENT DIAGRAM

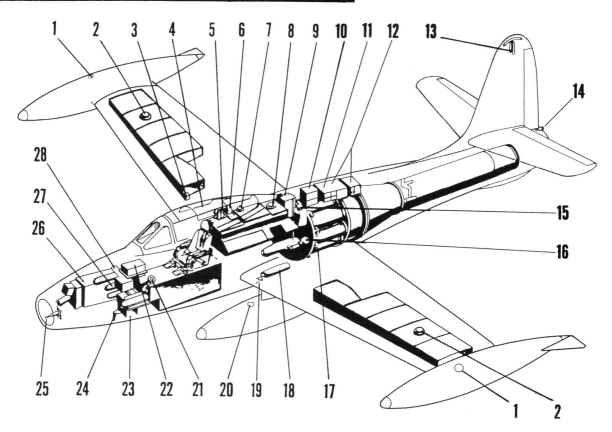

This general arrangement diagram illustrates and identifies the major features of the Thunderjet's design.
(USAFM)

1. WING TIP TANK FILLER
2. WING FUEL TANK FILLER
3. EXTERNAL POWER RECEPTACLE
4. RADIO COMPASS ANTENNA
5. COCKPIT PRESSURE REGULATOR
6. RADIO COMPASS LOOP ANTENNA
7. COCKPIT PRESSURE PUMP VALVE
8. MAIN FUEL TANK FILLER
9. ENGINE OIL TANK FILLER
10. IDENTIFICATION RADIO EQUIPMENT
11. RADIO COMPASS EQUIPMENT
12. COMMAND RADIO EQUIPMENT
13. COMMAND RADIO ANTENNA
14. POSITION LIGHT
15. HYDRAULIC OIL TANK FILLER
16. ALCOHOL TANK FILLER
17. JET ENGINE
18. HIGH PRESSURE OXYGEN BOTTLE
19. OXYGEN FILLER VALVE
    (SOME AIRPLANES)
20. PYLON TANK FILLER
21. FORWARD FUEL TANK FILLER
22. SIGHT COMPUTER EQUIPMENT
23. BATTERIES
24. BATTERY DRAIN JAR
25. PITOT TUBE
26. RADAR EQUIPMENT
27. LOW PRESSURE OXYGEN BOTTLES
28. OXYGEN FILLER VALVES

The problems experienced with the F-84B and F-84C, along with the resulting lack of operational readiness, caused sufficient concern within the Air Force that a special review of the Thunderjet program was conducted in September 1948. Consideration was given to cancelling the program, but because so much money had already been spent on the F-84D, it was decided to proceed with the delivery of the 154 aircraft already on order. But the Air Force directed that tests using F-84Ds be conducted at Wright Patterson Air Force Base, Ohio, and Eglin Air Force Base, Florida, it order to determine if the program should be continued. When these evaluations showed that many of the maintenance and serviceability problems experienced with the F-84B and F-84C had been corrected, the Air Force was encouraged. The tests also demonstrated that the F-84D was superior to the F-80 Shooting Star in most performance categories, and that it was the better fighter-bomber. As a result, Republic was permitted to carry on with the scheduled production of the F-84E.

The new jets also meant that pilots had to become familiar with completely different flying characteristics than they had known in propeller driven fighters. The accident rate due to pilot error had been very high, so the U. S. Air Force revised and intensified the training program to improve pilot awareness of the jets' characteristics and potential dangers. The new program proved to

An engine upgrade and a new electrical system differentiated the F-84C from the previous F-84B. Otherwise, there was no real difference between the first two production variants. *(USAFM)*

be quite successful, and accidents due to pilot error decreased significantly.

In order to keep the Thunderjet contract alive, Republic had been hard at work trying to correct the problems experienced with the early variants while enhancing the design at the same time. When the F-84E was first delivered in May 1949, the Thunderjet finally met the standards which the Air Force and Republic had originally intended.

The forward fuselage of the F-84E was lengthened by twelve inches to provide more room in the cockpit. Although it used the same J35-A-17 powerplant used in the F-84D, performance improved significantly. Its capabilities as a fighter-bomber were enhanced, and the fuel system was redesigned so that two 230-gallon drop tanks could be carried on jettisonable pylons beneath the wings. This increased its maximum range to almost 2,000 miles. A total of 843 F-84Es were delivered, of which 743 went to the U. S. Air Force and 100 were provided to NATO countries under the Mutual Defense

The F-84E was much improved over previous versions of the Thunderjet, and it was capable of higher speeds and increased "G" loads. The ability to carry under-wing stores was also expanded. *(USAFM)*

F-84Es also served with the Air National Guard. This Thunderjet was the first F-84E-15-RE produced, and it is shown here after being assigned to the Ohio Guard's 166th Fighter Squadron at Springfield. The markings are red, and the outline of the state of Ohio on the tail band is white. **(USAFM)**

Protection Program. This number easily exceeded the production of all earlier versions combined, and as the F-84Es became available, the F-84Bs, F-84Cs, and F-84Ds were turned over to Air National Guard Units. However, the persistent problems with these earlier variants also resulted in relatively quick retirement from the Guard.

The F-84E first went to Korea as the 27th Fighter Escort Wing deployed there in December 1950. A total of sixty Thunderjets were involved, and although other publications state that some F-84Ds were among the Thunderjets assigned to the 27th FEW at that time, the fact is that all were F-84Es. F-84Ds were sent to Korea as attrition replacements in early 1952, and most served with the Air National Guard's 136th Fighter Bomber Wing during its combat tour.

For a while after the F-84Es arrived in Korea, operational readiness suffered because of a critical shortage of spare parts. But the situation quickly improved, and the Thunderjets began to prove that they were clearly the best fighter-bomber the Air Force had in its inventory. By the end of the conflict, F-84Ds, F-84Es, and F-84Gs had flown 86,406 sorties, almost all of which were against targets on the ground. Only 144 were lost to enemy action, and of these, 135 were as the result of ground fire. This worked out to only one aircraft lost for every 640 sorties, and considering the intense fire they encountered while attacking heavily defended ground targets, this loss rate was truly amazing.

Even before the Korean War ended, F-84Es were replacing earlier versions in the Air National Guard where they remained in service until the last ones were phased out in 1959. Starting in 1954, F-84Es were also assigned to the Air Force Reserve where they continued in service until 1957.

The F-84G was the definitive and last version of the Thunderjet. It featured an in-flight refueling capability compatable with both the flying boom and the probe and drogue systems. It also was the first production fighter-bomber capable of delivering an atomic weapon. This F-84G-1-RE was assigned to the 523rd Fighter Escort Squadron of the 27th Fighter Escort Wing. The photograph was taken at Misawa Air Base, Japan, on October 13, 1952. The markings on the nose, tip tanks, and vertical tail are yellow. **(USAFM)**

Although not able to compete with the MiG-15 in air-to-air combat, the Thunderjet became the U. S. Air Force's premier fighter-bomber during the Korean War. Loaded with two 500-pound bombs, this F-84G from the 58th Fighter Bomber Group takes off for a mission against the communists on January 21, 1953. (USAFM)

The F-84F designation was assigned to a swept wing development of the Thunderjet which was named the Thunderstreak. From it, a swept wing reconnaissance version, known as the Thunderflash and designated RF-84F, was also developed. These aircraft did not become operational until after the F-84G, and they are beyond the scope of this book.

The final development of the Thunderjet series was the F-84G. Its noticeable improvements over the F-84E included an uprated J35-A-29 powerplant with an additional 600 pounds of trust. This pushed the performance capabilities to the limit that could be achieved with the conventional straight wing design, and it permitted heavier loads of external stores to be carried. To correct one continuing structural problem, the F-84G had a reinforced canopy as a production standard, and this was also retrofitted to all earlier versions remaining in service.

Experiments conducted with two EF-84Es had demonstrated the capability of installing in-flight refueling systems in fighter aircraft. The F-84G became the first fighter-bomber to be produced with in-flight refueling equipment. A receptacle was installed in the left wing near the root, and it was covered by two triangular shaped doors when not in use. This receptacle was compatible with the flying boom system preferred by the Strategic Air Command and designed for its new jet bombers. At that time, many tankers could only use the probe and drogue method of in-flight refueling, so probes were installed on the inboard side at the front of tip tanks. When tanks with these probes were installed, the F-84G could refuel using either system. Tip tanks with

the probes were also retrofitted to some F-84Es which were flown by the Air National Guard's 116th Fighter Bomber Wing. Because tankers operating in the Far East used the probe and drogue system, F-84Gs deployed to Korea were often provided with the tip tanks which had the probes installed.

The ability to refuel in flight meant that large numbers of fighters could quickly be flown to anywhere they were needed in the world. Operations Fox Peter One and Fox Peter Two involved deployments of the 31st Fighter Escort Wing and the 27th Fighter Escort Wing respectively to the Far East during 1952. In August of the following year, seventeen F-84Gs from the 508th Fighter Escort Wing flew 4,485 miles from Turner Air Force Base, Georgia, to Bentwaters Royal Air Base, England. This was the longest non-stop deployment of fighter aircraft up until that time. As the F-84Gs of the 508th FEW flew to England, Thunderjets of the 31st Fighter

Far more F-84Gs were produced for the air forces of foreign nations under the Military Assistance Program than were delivered to the U. S. Air Force. These F-84Gs fly in the markings of the Norwegian Air Force. (USAFM)

MAIN DIFFERENCES TABLE   *F-84B through F-84G*

AIRPLANE	F-84B	F-84C	F-84D	F-84E	F-84G
ENGINE	J35-C-3 J35-A-5 J35-A-15	J35-A-13	J35-A-17 Derated J35-A-29	J35-A-17	J35-A-29A
FUEL SYSTEM CONTROLS	Toggle switches up to F-84B-21RE	Rotary switch F-84B-21RE up to F-84C-11RE	Manual Fuel tank selector F-84C-11RE and up	Manual Fuel tank selector	Manual Fuel tank selector
LANDING GEAR	Hydraulic Shrink Struts	Hydraulic Shrink Struts	Mechanical Shrink Struts	Mechanical Shrink Struts	Mechanical Shrink Struts
TRIM TABS	Conventional	Conventional	Conventional	Left aileron and elevators only	Left aileron and elevators only
CANOPY	Jettison	Jettison	Jettison with canopy remover	Jettison with canopy remover	Jettison with canopy remover
GUN SIGHT	K-14B	K-14B	A-1C	A-1C with APG-30 provisions	A-1CM or A-4 with APG-30 or MK-18
BOMB RACKS	Fixed Pylon	Fixed Pylon	Fixed Pylon	Jettisonable pylon	Jettisonable pylon

This table was taken from the F-84G's "dash one" manual, and it summarizes the main differences between the production versions of the Thunderjet. (USAFM)

Escort Wing also took off from Turner Air Force base and flew to Sidi Slimane Air Base, French Morocco. This simultaneous long range movement of F-84Gs from two different wings was called Operation Longstride. In May 1955, F-84Gs of the 49th Fighter Bomber Wing established a new record of 4,840 miles when they flew nonstop from Tokyo, Japan, to Newcastle, Australia. These early long range deployments were the first demonstrations of the value of in-flight refueling for fighter aircraft, but today it is taken for granted that all U. S. fighters have this essential capability.

The F-84G was also the first fighter sized aircraft capable of delivering a tactical atomic weapon. This meant that the U. S. Air Force did not have to rely solely on large bombers to carry atomic weapons. Therefore, any potential enemy was faced with a far more complex and versatile atomic capability against which it was very difficult to defend. Because of this, the ability of fighters to deliver nuclear weapons also significantly contributed to the credibility of deterrence which helped maintain the peace during the cold war.

A total of 3,025 F-84Gs were produced, but only 789 of these served with the U. S. Air Force. The other 2,236 were sent to thirteen different foreign nations under the Mutual Defense Assistance Program which was later renamed the Military Assistance Program. The total number of Thunderjets produced was 4,457, more than

any other American combat jet aircraft up to that time. SAC retired its F-84Gs in 1955 but some remained in the inventory of the Tactical Air Command until the early 1960s.

There is no question that early production versions of the Thunderjet were plagued with a multitude of problems that almost ended the program prematurely. There were structural deficiencies that had to be worked out, maintenance was a nightmare, developing and sustaining an effective logistical supply system was quite difficult at first, and both pilots and ground crew personnel had to become proficient with an aircraft that was considerably different than anything they had seen before. From the design stage to combat, the new jets were a world apart from the previous propeller driven fighters that they had so quickly replaced. It therefore should not have come as any surprise that serious difficulties would be encountered as the major transition was made in technology, operations, training, maintenance, and logistics. By the time the F-84E and F-84G were delivered, the Air Force and Republic had worked hard to correct the initial deficiencies, and they had been very successful in every area.

In Korea, the Thunderjet became known as the "champ of all low level bombers" and the "workhorse of the Korean War." It was not the sleek steed flown by the aces in Mig Alley, but it performed the essential fighter-bomber role remarkably well. In doing so it carried on the tradition established by the P-47 Thunderbolt during World War II, and it set the stage for the F-105 Thunderchief that proved to be an excellent fighter-bomber during the war in Vietnam over a decade later.

THUNDERJET VARIANTS
XP-84

When it was initially rolled out, the first of three XP-84 experimental prototypes was completely unpainted and devoid of any markings. Notice the pitot boom located near the midpoint on the leading edge of the left wing.
(USAFM)

The three XP-84 prototypes were included in the initial letter contract issued to Republic on November 11, 1944. An inspection of the mock-up for the design was held in February 1945, and when the Army judged it to be satisfactory, a formal cost-plus-fixed-fee contract was issued on March 12, 1945.

The first of the three XP-84s, serial number 45-59475, was rolled out of Republic's plant at Farmingdale, New York, in December 1945. At that time, it was unpainted natural metal and completely devoid of any markings. Shortly thereafter, it was painted in an overall light gray paint scheme with black serial numbers on each side of the vertical tail. The buzz number, consisting of **PS-**

plus the last three digits of the aircraft's serial number, was painted in black on both sides of the forward fuselage and the underside of the left wing. The blue and white national insignia, standard for that time frame, was applied to both sides of the aft fuselage, the top of the left wing, and the bottom of the right wing.

After being shipped across the country to Muroc Flight Test Base, California (now Edwards Air Force Base), the prototype was prepared for its maiden flight. With Major Wallace Lein at the controls, it took to the air for the first time on February 28, 1946. It was immediately evident that performance was superior to that of Lockheed's P-80 Shooting Star, and the second prototype, 45-59476, which began flying in August 1946, set

The aircraft was soon painted in an overall light gray paint scheme with black lettering. The national insignia without the red stripes was standard at the time the XP-84s first flew.
(USAFM)

Above: An in-flight photograph clearly illustrates the very simple lines of the XP-84. Note the antenna under the forward fuselage. (USAFM)

Right: All versions of the Thunderjet had a sliding bubble canopy. Problems with the canopy would cause reinforcing strips to be added on later variants. Many earlier aircraft would also have canopies with these strips retrofitted. (USAFM)

a U. S. speed record of 611 miles-per-hour on September 7th. Both of these prototypes were fitted with the J35-GE-7 engine which produced only 3,750 pounds of thrust. The third prototype, 45-59477, had an Allison-built J35-A-15 which delivered 4,000 pounds of thrust. As a result of this engine change and several additional design modifications, it was redesignated XP-84A.

Although the performance of the XP-84 was encouraging, there were also some critical problems that had to be overcome. Wind tunnel and flight testing had revealed some stability deficiencies, and the airframe was overweight. Both the Army Air Force and Republic realized that these had to be corrected if the program was to continue.

The three prototypes were unique in that they were painted in a light gray paint scheme. All subsequent aircraft were unpainted natural metal. The XP-84s also had a long pitot boom on the leading edge of the left wing, and this was also a feature unique to these three aircraft. None of the prototypes were fitted with the tip tanks that would soon become standard on production aircraft.

XP-84 1/72nd SCALE DRAWING

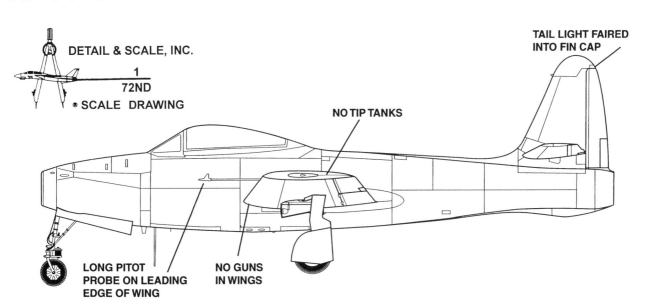

DETAIL & SCALE, INC.

$\frac{1}{72ND}$

® SCALE DRAWING

TAIL LIGHT FAIRED INTO FIN CAP

NO TIP TANKS

LONG PITOT PROBE ON LEADING EDGE OF WING

NO GUNS IN WINGS

DETAIL & SCALE, 1/72nd SCALE, COPYRIGHT © DRAWING BY LLOYD JONES

YP-84A

The seventh of the fifteen YP-84A-REs is shown during a publicity flight for Republic. The long pitot boom on the left wing has been replaced with a short one on the vertical tail. Also note the change in the style of the national insignia with the red stripe inside the rectangles. The PS prefix to the buzz number indicates the continued use of the pursuit designation at the time the YP-84As were being used for flight evaluation.   (USAFM)

The original contract called for twenty-five service test aircraft, but this was subsequently reduced to fifteen. Designated YP-84As, they were divided into three production blocks as follows:

YP-84A-1-RE . . . . 45-59482 through 45-59484
YP-84A-5-RE . . . . 45-59485 through 45-59491
YP-84A-10-RE . . . . 45-59492 through 45-49496.

They were similar to the two XP-84s and one XP-84A except that the long pitot probe on the left wing was replaced by a short unit on the leading edge of the vertical stabilizer. Provisions for tip tanks were included in the design, but there is no evidence that these were ever fitted. Because the gray paint applied to the XP-84s had peeled off at high speeds, the YP-84As were unpainted natural metal. All fifteen were powered with the Allison J35-A-15 engine which delivered 4,000 pounds of thrust. Internal armament was added in the form of six .50-caliber M2 machine guns, with four being located in the nose above the engine inlet, and the other two being mounted in the wing roots. This armament would remain standard for all Thunderjet variants that followed.

Deliveries of the fifteen test aircraft were made during February 1947, with all of the YP-84As being used for flight test purposes at Muroc Flight Test Center and Wright Field, Ohio. Performance data for the YP-84A was essentially the same as for the F-84B as provided on the following page.

The fourteenth YP-84A looks very much like the production P-84Bs that followed, however none of the YP-84As were fitted with tip tanks.   *(USAFM)*

F-84B

This well known shot of two P-84Bs in flight was actually a publicity photograph. "Republic P-84 Thunderjet" was lettered in red on the side of the fuselage of each aircraft. The P-84B was the first version of the Thunderjet to be fitted with tip tanks. **(USAFM)**

The first production version of the Thunderjet was the P-84B which differed little from the fifteen YP-84A service test aircraft. The only noteworthy change was that the M2 machine guns were replaced by M3 weapons that offered an increased rate of fire. Starting with the eighty-sixth P-84B, the capability to carry 5-inch HVAR rockets was added to supplement the machine gun armament. The provisions for carrying tip tanks was first put to use on the P-84B, and although these tanks were usually carried, it was not uncommon to see P-84Bs without them. Deliveries of the 226 P-84Bs began in June 1947 and continued through June 1948.

In 1947, the U. S. Air Force became a separate branch of the service, and they changed the pursuit classification to fighter on June 11, 1948. As a result, the P-84 designation became F-84, and the **PS**- prefix in the buzz number was changed to **FS**-. Other changes in markings on the aircraft included a deletion of the buzz number under the left wing and a large **USAF** was added with Insignia Blue paint on the bottom of the left wing and the top of the right. In much smaller letters, **U. S. AIR FORCE** was added in black above the serial number on the tail.

Early problems, first noticed with the YP-84s during testing, continued to plague the Thunderjet after it entered service with the 14th Fighter Group at Dow Field, Maine. Most critical was that the skin of the aircraft wrinkled at high speeds, so speed and acceleration limitations had to be placed on them. Even so, in May 1948, the entire fleet of P-84Bs was grounded for inspection due to structural failures, and a modification program costing eight million dollars had to be implemented to strengthen the airframes. By the time these improvements had been completed, the designation change from pursuit to fighter had been made, but the F-84Bs returned to service with Air Force squadrons for a short period of time before being transferred to the Air National Guard.

DATA

Version	F-84B
Number Built	226
Powerplant	Allison J35-A-15C
Static Thrust	4,000 pounds
Maximum Speed	587 mph
Cruising Speed	436 mph
Climb in One Minute	5,200 feet
Ceiling	40,750 feet
Range	1,282 miles
Internal Fuel Capacity	416 gallons
Total Fuel Capacity	786 gallons
Empty Weight	9,538 pounds
Maximum Gross Take-off Weight	19,689 pounds

P-84Bs often operated without their tip tanks. Careful examination of this photograph will reveal that the buzz number was painted under the left wing. This was standard practice until the United States Air Force was formed in September 1947. The early style landing gear with the hydraulic shrink struts is visible in this photograph and the one below. (USAFM)

Above: This P-84B was named "Itsy Bitsy III," and it was the personal aircraft of Lt. Col. George Laven. The aircraft was assigned to the 49th Fighter Squadron of the 14th Fighter Group. (USAFM)

Right: The change from the pursuit designation to fighter is exemplified by the FS prefix in the buzz number of "Virginia S," an F-84B from the 20th Fighter Bomber Group at Shaw Air Force Base, South Carolina. It was flown by Lt. L. A. Carlson. Also note that U. S. AIR FORCE has been lettered on the vertical tail. When these changes were made, USAF replaced the buzz number on the underside of the left wing, and it was added to the top of the right wing. (USAFM)

Some F-84Bs were eventually assigned to Air National Guard units. This F-84B-3-RE was flown by the 116th Fighter Squadron of the Washington ANG, and this photograph proves that even these early Thunderjets were retrofitted with reinforced canopies late in their service life. *(USAFM)*

Details on the instrument panel in F-84B-21-RE, 46-533, are illustrated in this photograph. *(USAFM)*

F-84B THUNDERJET DIMENSIONS

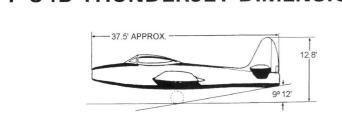

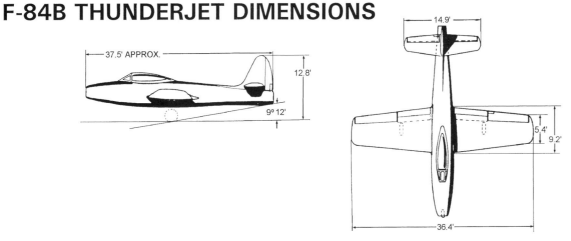

F-84B, 1/72nd SCALE, FIVE-VIEW DRAWINGS

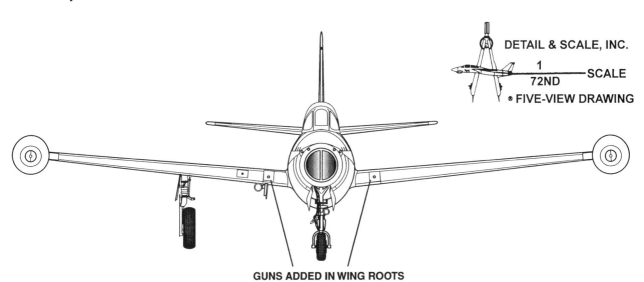

DETAIL & SCALE, INC.

$\dfrac{1}{72\text{ND}}$ SCALE

® FIVE-VIEW DRAWING

GUNS ADDED IN WING ROOTS

DETAIL & SCALE, 1/72nd SCALE, COPYRIGHT © DRAWING BY LLOYD JONES

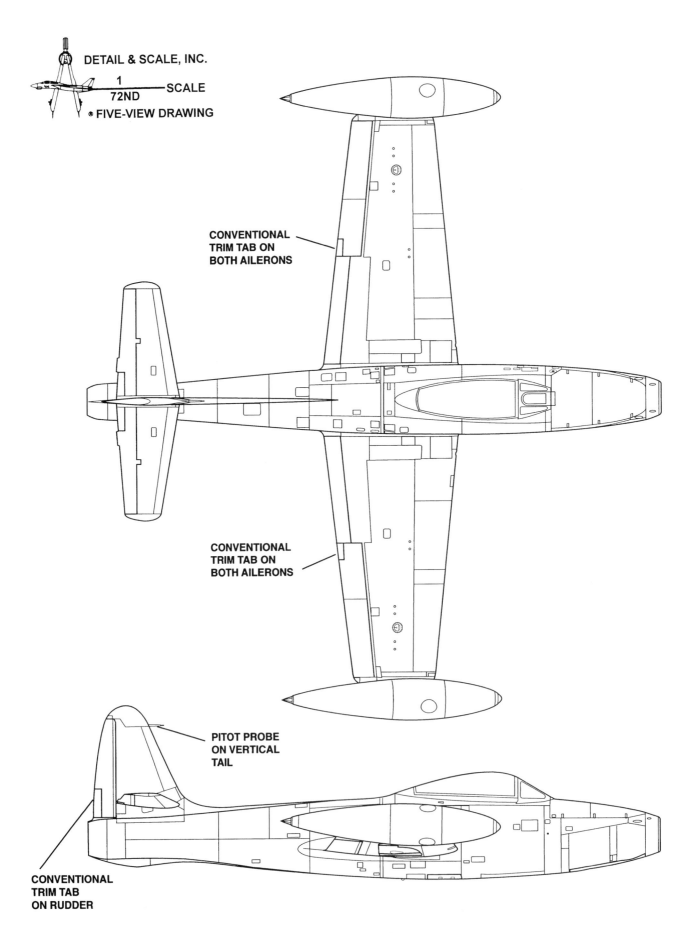

DETAIL & SCALE, INC.

$\dfrac{1}{72ND}$ SCALE

® FIVE-VIEW DRAWING

CONVENTIONAL
TRIM TAB ON
BOTH AILERONS

CONVENTIONAL
TRIM TAB ON
BOTH AILERONS

PITOT PROBE
ON VERTICAL
TAIL

CONVENTIONAL
TRIM TAB
ON RUDDER

DETAIL & SCALE, 1/72nd SCALE, COPYRIGHT © DRAWING BY LLOYD JONES

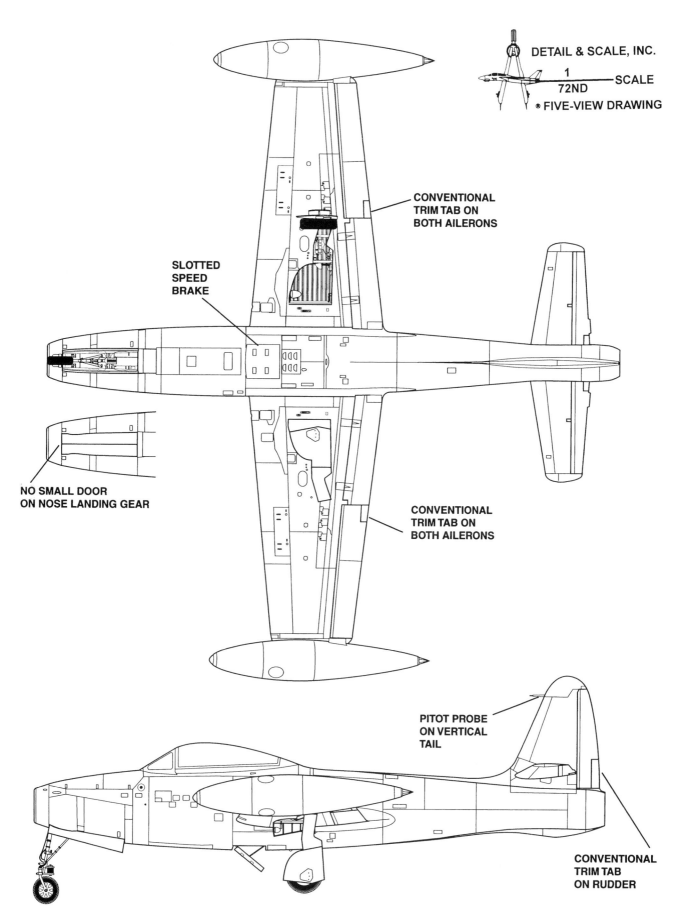

DETAIL & SCALE, INC.

SCALE
1
72ND

® FIVE-VIEW DRAWING

CONVENTIONAL
TRIM TAB ON
BOTH AILERONS

SLOTTED
SPEED
BRAKE

NO SMALL DOOR
ON NOSE LANDING GEAR

CONVENTIONAL
TRIM TAB ON
BOTH AILERONS

PITOT PROBE
ON VERTICAL
TAIL

CONVENTIONAL
TRIM TAB
ON RUDDER

DETAIL & SCALE, 1/72nd SCALE, COPYRIGHT © DRAWING BY LLOYD JONES

F-84C

An uprated engine and an improved electrical system were the only real changes found in the F-84C. Its exterior appearance was identical to the previous F-84B, and like the "B-model," it was not uncommon to see F-84Cs without their tip tanks. This F-84C has the original canopy without the reinforcing strips. (USAFM)

The F-84C differed little from the F-84B that preceded it on the production line. The only significant changes were an improved electrical system and an engine model change. The J35-A-15C, used in the YP-84A and the F-84B, was replaced with the J35-A-13C which produced the same 4,000 pounds of thrust. Maximum and cruising speeds remained the same as they had been for the F-84B, but a slightly heavier weight resulted in a marginally slower rate of climb. Maximum range also decreased slightly because of the additional weight.

Because the airframe of the F-84C was essentially the same as that used for the F-84B, the structural problems were experienced with this variant of the Thunderjet as well. Therefore, the same airframe modification pro-

gram had to be implemented to make the F-84C airworthy throughout its entire flight envelope. Deliveries began in May 1948, and the entire production run of 191 aircraft had been completed by the following November.

The 33rd Fighter Group, first at Kirtland Air Force Base, New Mexico, then at Otis Air Force Base, Maine, was the first unit to receive the F-84C. The only other Air Force group to become operational in the F-84Cs was the 31st Fighter Group at Albany, Georgia. Contrary to what has been published elsewhere, neither the 20th Fighter Group at Shaw Air Force Base, South Carolina, nor the 78th Fighter Group at Hamilton Air Force Base, California, ever attained an operational status with the F-84C, although a few "C-models" may have been used by one or both of these units as instructional airframes. Like the F-84B, the F-84C remained in service with the Air Force for a relatively short period of time before being turned over to the Air National Guard and replaced with later variants. By the end of 1952, all F-84Bs and F-84Cs had also been retired from service with the Guard as well.

F-84Cs only served for a few years with the Air National Guard after they were replaced by later variants in the regular Air Force. F-84C-11-RE, 47-1537, has markings for the West Virginia ANG. (USAFM)

DATA

Version	F-84C
Number Built	191
Powerplant	Allison J35-A-13C
Static Thrust	4,000 pounds
Maximum Speed	587 mph
Cruising Speed	436 mph
Climb in One Minute	4,180 feet
Ceiling	40,600 feet
Range	1,274 miles
Internal Fuel Capacity	416 gallons
Total Fuel Capacity	786 gallons
Empty Weight	9,662 pounds
Maximum Gross Take-off Weight	19,798 pounds

Above: Once they were retired from flying status, early versions of the Thunderjet were sometimes used for ground training purposes. F-84C-16-RE, 47-1580, has markings for the Illinois Guard where it was used as an instructional airframe. The fins on the tip tanks were not originally installed on F-84Cs, but they were later retro-fitted. *(USAFM)*

Right: The instrument panel in the F-84C differed very little from that in the F-84B. *(USAFM)*

Major items on the left side of the cockpit included the throttle stand, armament control switches, tab control switches, the flap lever, and fuel tank indicators and controls. The large item with the hose at the aft end of the console is the valve for the anti-G suit. *(USAFM)*

Features found on the right side of the cockpit included the radio control panel, map case, and map reading light. These stepped consoles were common to early Thunderjets with the shorter fuselage and cockpit. This included all variants through the F-84D. *(USAFM)*

F-84D

The F-84D was structurally strengthened, and a thicker gauge of metal was used to skin the wings. A noticeable visible change was that the pitot probe was moved from the leading edge of the vertical tail to the splitter inside the engine inlet in the nose. This F-84D-10-RE was assigned to the 79th Fighter Bomber Squadron of the 20th Fighter Bomber Group at Shaw Air Force Base, South Carolina, in 1950. (Norm Taylor collection via USAFM)

The F-84D was the first version of the Thunderjet to be truly operationally ready for combat. The structural components of the airframe were strengthened, and the skin on the wing was increased to a thicker gauge. Small fins were added to the outboard aft end of the tip tanks to prevent them from twisting at high speeds, and this eliminated one of the sources of structural problems that had been experienced on earlier variants. Another noticeable physical change was that the pitot probe was moved from the leading edge of the vertical tail to the air flow splitter inside the engine inlet.

The landing gear was also changed to one with mechanical shrink struts instead of the hydraulic type used previously. Internally, the F-84D had a winterized fuel system which could use JP4 fuel, and a manual fuel tank selector, first installed in the F-84C-11-RE, became a production standard. The K-14B gun sight was replaced with an A-1B unit, and this was subsequently upgraded to an A-1C. The canopy was equipped with a device known as a remover to facilitate a hasty exit in the event of an emergency. Other improvements were made to simplify maintenance access and to increase reliability. Among these improvements was a cover for the gun bay in the nose that was hinged at the forward end. This replaced the cover on earlier Thunderjets that had to be removed completely to gain access to the weapons.

Although lighter fuel cells were installed to decrease weight, the net effect of these changes contributed to an increase in empty weight of approximately two-hundred pounds. Yet the overall performance of the F-84D was still equal to that of the F-84B and F-84C in most categories, because the J35-A-17 engine used in the F-84D produced 5,000 pounds of thrust compared to the 4,000 pounds available in the two earlier production versions. Cruising speed and rate of climb actually increased slightly, while rate of climb and range were only marginally reduced.

Deliveries of the F-84D began in November 1948, and 154 were completed by April of the following year. This was the fewest number of any production variant of the Thunderjet, because the much improved F-84E was ready to replace it on the assembly line the following month.

In September 1948, the Air Force conducted a review of the entire Thunderjet program and concluded that neither the F-84B or F-84C could satisfactorily meet operational mission requirements. Because significant funds had already been spent on the F-84D, it was decided to continue with its procurement, but any further investment in continuing the program was clearly in jeopardy. To help decide what action to take, the Air Force ordered that tests be conducted at Eglin Air Force Base, Florida, and Wright Patterson Air Force Base, Ohio. These tests, conducted in February and March 1949, revealed that many of the shortcomings present in the previous Thunderjet variants had been corrected in the F-84D. Further, when flown against the F-80 Shooting Star, the F-84D proved to be superior in range, acceleration, versatility, load carrying capability, high altitude climb, and speed in level flight. The F-80 was better when it came to takeoff distance, low altitude climb, and maneuverability. The overall scorecard was in favor of the F-84D, and the Air Force was encouraged enough to continue with the program.

Contrary to what has been stated in at least two other publications, F-84Ds were not deployed with the 27th Fighter Escort Wing when that unit was sent to Korea in December 1950. At that time, the 27th FEW was equipped entirely with F-84Es. However, F-84Ds were sent to Korea as attrition replacements in early 1952 to serve primarily with the Air National Guard's 136th Fighter Bomber Group.

Although it was superior in most respects to the Lockheed F-80 Shooting Star, and it proved capable of

The "Flying Yankees" of the Connecticut Air National Guard's 118th Fighter Squadron flew F-84Ds. The unit insignia appears on the nose of the aircraft, and FLY SAFELY is lettered within the markings on the tip tanks. Also note the stabilizing fin on the tip tanks. These were added during production of the F-84D and were also retrofitted to earlier aircraft. **(USAFM)**

flying combat missions in Korea, the F-84D still did not completely meet the standards of performance that the Air Force had hoped for. By 1953, after the much improved F-84E had become available, most had been transferred to the Air National Guard where they remained in service until the last F-84Ds were retired in mid-1957.

DATA

Version	F-84D
Number Built	154
Powerplant	Allison J35-A-17
Static Thrust	5,000 pounds
Maximum Speed	587 mph
Cruising Speed	441 mph
Climb in One Minute	4,600 feet
Ceiling	39,300 feet
Range	1,198 miles
Internal Fuel Capacity	416 gallons
Total Fuel Capacity	786 gallons
Empty Weight	9,860 pounds
Maximum Gross Take-off Weight	20,076 pounds

F-84D 1/72nd SCALE DRAWING

DETAIL & SCALE, INC.

$$\frac{1}{72ND}$$

® SCALE DRAWING

PITOT PROBE MOVED FROM VERTICAL TAIL TO INLET SPLITTER

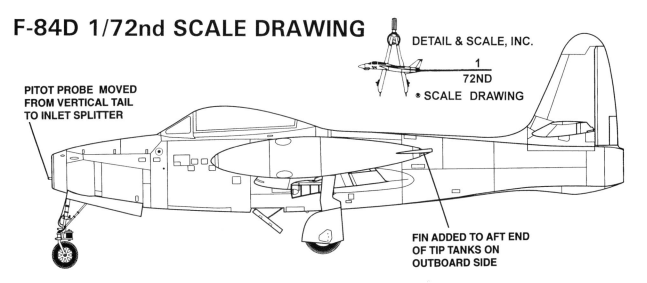

FIN ADDED TO AFT END OF TIP TANKS ON OUTBOARD SIDE

DETAIL & SCALE, 1/72nd SCALE, COPYRIGHT © DRAWING BY LLOYD JONES

F-84E

The F-84E was much improved over all previous versions of the Thunderjet, and it had a fuselage that was lengthened by twelve inches to provide more room in the cockpit. **(USAFM)**

The F-84E was a considerable improvement over the F-84D, and with its introduction into operational service, the Air Force finally had a version of the Thunderjet that possessed the capabilities it wanted. Because it was now understood that the straight wing F-84 could not compete in air-to-air combat with swept wing fighters like the F-86 and MiG-15, the F-84E was optimized to serve as a fighter bomber. Tests at Wright Patterson Air Force Base indicated that serviceability and ease of main-

tenance was finally up to acceptable standards, thus eliminating problems that had plagued all of the earlier versions of the aircraft. Problems did still persist with the A-1B gun sight, and it was replaced with the modified A-1C. Provisions were also included for the APG-30

Beginning with the F-84E, the tip tanks were redesigned to make them better able to withstand the rigors of combat. The fuel system was modified so that two 230-gallon drop tanks could be carried on pylons under each wing inboard of the landing gear as seen on this F-84E-5-RE. This significantly increased the combat radius of the aircraft. Alternatively, several different types of ordnance could also be carried on these pylons. **(USAFM)**

The colorful checkerboard markings of Col. George Laven's F-84E-30-RE are reflected in the melting snow at Landsuhl Air Base, Germany, which is the present day Ramstein Air Base. The aircraft was assigned to the 86th Fighter Group which Laven commanded. (USAFM)

radar gun sight.

The length of the forward fuselage of the F-84E was increased by twelve inches to provide more room in the cockpit and improve pilot comfort. Jettisonable pylons were added under each wing inboard of the landing gear to carry ordnance or external fuel tanks. This raised the total fuel capacity to 1,372 gallons, and as a result, the maximum range increased to 1,950 miles. The wing structure was strengthened to withstand increased G-loads, and the tip tanks were redesigned to better handle the rigors of combat. A noticeable fairing was placed all the way around each tank to cover the seam where the halves were joined. Vents at the rear of the tanks and on each side of the aft fuselage permitted fuel to be jettisoned quickly when it was necessary to lighten the aircraft.

The flight control system was also redesigned, and the conventional trim tabs were removed from the rudder and right aileron. These were replaced with fixed balance tabs. Trim tabs remained only on the left aileron and the elevators. The rear position light was moved from its location near the top of the trailing edge of the vertical tail to a small fairing just below the base of the rudder.

In spite of the fact that the F-84E was fitted with the same J35-A-17 powerplant used in the F-84D, performance increased significantly because of the redesigned airframe which provided for a more efficient air flow. Top speed rose to 613 miles-per-hour while crusing speed was 481 miles-per-hour. Initial rate of climb im-

proved by 2,000 feet-per-minute, and the service ceiling increased to 43,220 feet. The excessively long takeoff run required to get the Thunderjet airborne led to the addition of a JATO (Jet Assisted TakeOff) capability in the F-84E. Two small bottles could be attached under the aft fuselage to provide additional thrust to get the aircraft airborne faster, particularly when it was loaded with external stores in the form of ordnance or fuel tanks. Technically, the units were actually rockets rather than jets, but the acronym JATO was preferred over the less common RATO.

Deliveries of the F-84E began in May 1949 and continued through July 1951. A total of 843 were produced, with 743 going to the U. S. Air Force and 100 being procured for the Mutual Defense Assistance Program. F-84Es delivered under MDAP, along with addi-

F-84Es of the 36th Fighter Bomber Group line the apron at Furstenfeldbruck Air Base, Germany. Note that these aircraft have the original canopy which did not have the reinforcing strips. (USAFM)

This F-84E-15-RE was assigned to the 10th Air Force which was part of the Air Force Reserves during the mid-1950s. Note that the buzz number has been moved to the aft fuselage and U. S. AIR FORCE has been lettered on the nose with Insignia Blue paint. (USAFM)

tional aircraft that were transferred to foreign nations after their service with the U. S. Air Force had been completed, were operated by Belgium, Denmark, France, The Netherlands, and Norway.

F-84Es equipped the 27th Fighter Escort Wing when that unit deployed to Korea in December 1950. Although a shortage of spare parts continued to plague the operational readiness of these Thunderjets, they proved to be the best fighter-bomber aircraft in the Air Force inventory. Pilots reported that the aircraft was exceptionally stable making it an excellent gun platform and increasing its accuracy in delivering bombs and rockets. After the war, the F-84E remained in the inventory of the Tactical Air Command until 1956, although many were retained only for training purposes. The Air Force Reserve flew F-84Es from 1954 through 1957, while the Air National Guard operated them from 1951 until 1959.

DATA

Version	F-84E
Number Built	843*
Powerplant	Allison J35-A-17
Static Thrust	5,000 pounds
Maximum Speed	613 mph
Cruising Speed	481 mph
Climb in One Minute	6,061 feet
Ceiling	43,200 feet
Range	1,950 miles**
Internal Fuel Capacity	452 gallons
Total Fuel Capacity	1,372 gallons
Empty Weight	10,205 pounds
Maximum Gross Take-off Weight	22,463 pounds

*743 for the U. S. Air Force and 100 for MDAP
**with external fuel tanks

F-84Es also saw considerable service with the Air National Guard. These Thunderjets were operated by the Ohio ANG which used red markings on its aircraft.
(USAFM)

F-84E COCKPIT DETAILS

With the rear view mirror tilted to a horizontal position, details of the gun sight are visible. (USAFM)

This close-up provides a good look at the instruments on the main panel. At the very center of the panel is the basic needle and ball, while directly above it is the directional gyroscopic compass. The magnetic standby compass is on the upper panel just to the right of center, and the artificial horizon is to the right of the directional gyro. Other basic flying instruments, such as the altimeter, rate-of-climb indicator, and airspeed indicator are also grouped at the center of the panel. (USAFM)

The increased fuselage length of the F-84E meant an extensive redesign of the cockpit. The instrument panel was considerably different than that found in previous versions of the Thunderjet. The photographs on this page were taken in the cockpit of F-84E-10-RE, 49-2292. Note the rear view mirror attached to the upper framework of the windscreen in this overall view. (USAFM)

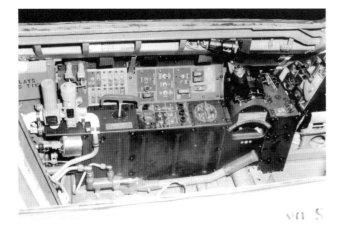

The left console was completely redesigned from that found in earlier variants of the Thunderjet, although the functions of the items included on it remained basically the same. Most noticeable is the throttle quadrant with the fuel selector switch just aft of it. The armament switches, fire extinguisher handle, and anti-G suit valve are all located on this side of the cockpit. (USAFM)

The major item on the right console was the radio panel near its center. Circuit breakers were located on the side of the console near the cockpit floor, and the map case and fuse identification placard are at the rear of the console. A map light is connected to a coiled cord on the side of the cockpit above the console. (USAFM)

Part of the FICON program to develop a parasite fighter that could be carried by bombers over long ranges was conducted with an F-84E. The Thunderjet could be carried under the fuselage of a B-36 bomber, then launched from a trapeze arrangement to provide fighter escort as shown here. Modified RF-84Fs, redesignated RF-84Ks, were also used in this program. *(USAFM)*

The F-84E was placed on a loading dolly when it was ready to be fitted onto the trapeze beneath the bomber. The program to develop parasite fighters did not prove to be very promising, and it was subsequently abandoned when in-flight refueling proved to be a far more practical means of providing long range fighter escort. *(USAFM)*

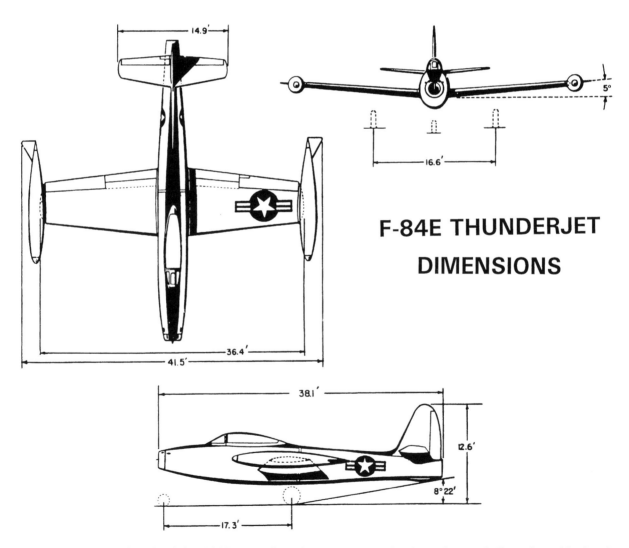

F-84E THUNDERJET
DIMENSIONS

The increased fuselage length of the F-84E, as well as the span across the tip tanks, are indicated on this drawing from the pilot's manual for the Thunderjet. The dimensions shown here would also apply to the F-84G. *(USAFM)*

A significant experiment involving F-84Es was this test conducted in late 1950. Two aircraft, redesignated EF-84Es, were fitted with an in-flight refueling probe installed in the leading edge of their left wing. Operating with a British Tanker, they set off on a trans-Atlantic flight from England to the United States, and although Lt. Col. William Ricthie had to bail out over Newfoundland, famous World War II ace, Col. David C. Schilling, completed the entire flight. This lead to the development of air-to-air refueling for fighter aircraft including the F-84G and some F-84Es with retrofitted refueling probes installed in their tip tanks. *(USAFM)*

Col. David Schilling maneuvers his EF-84E into the basket behind the British tanker. Note the location of the probe on the leading edge of the wing. Later, these probes would be installed directly into the tip tanks of some operational F-84Es and F-84Gs on the inboard side near the front. The F-84G was produced with a receptacle in the leading edge of the left wing for use with the flying boom in-flight refueling system preferred by the U. S. Air Force. (See page 53.) The development of in-flight refueling for fighters was quite significant, because it meant that large numbers of fighters could be deployed anywhere in the world quickly and easily. *(USAFM)*

F-84E, 1/72nd SCALE, FIVE-VIEW DRAWINGS

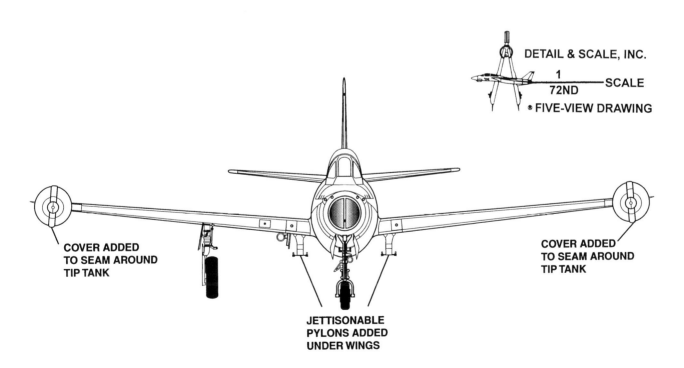

DETAIL & SCALE, INC.

$\dfrac{1}{72\text{ND}}$ SCALE

® FIVE-VIEW DRAWING

COVER ADDED
TO SEAM AROUND
TIP TANK

COVER ADDED
TO SEAM AROUND
TIP TANK

JETTISONABLE
PYLONS ADDED
UNDER WINGS

DETAIL & SCALE, 1/72nd SCALE, COPYRIGHT © DRAWING BY LLOYD JONES

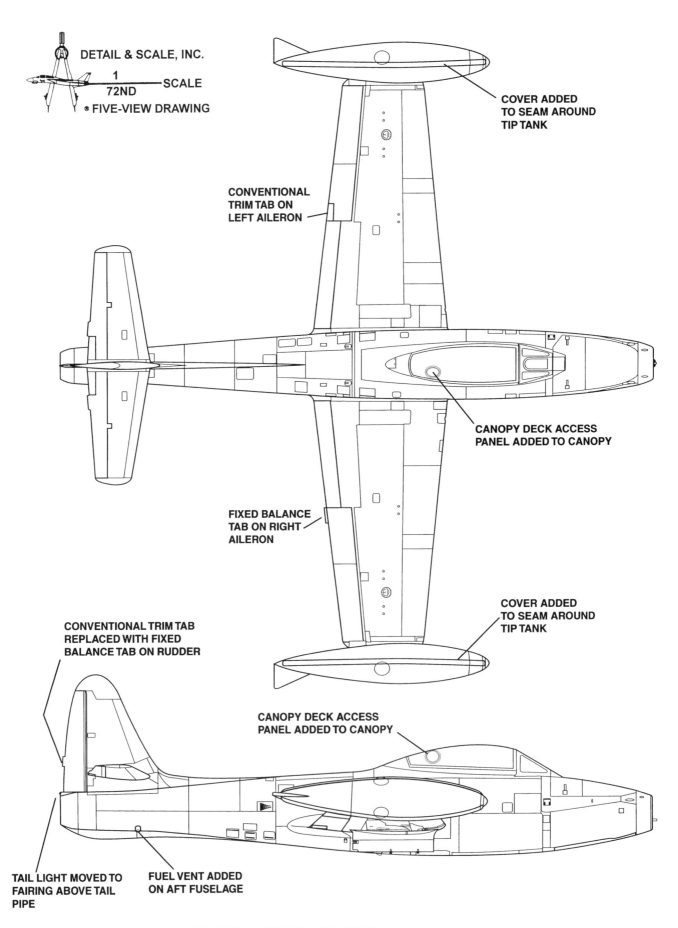

DETAIL & SCALE, INC.

$\frac{1}{72ND}$ —— SCALE

® FIVE-VIEW DRAWING

COVER ADDED
TO SEAM AROUND
TIP TANK

CONVENTIONAL
TRIM TAB ON
LEFT AILERON

CANOPY DECK ACCESS
PANEL ADDED TO CANOPY

FIXED BALANCE
TAB ON RIGHT
AILERON

COVER ADDED
TO SEAM AROUND
TIP TANK

CONVENTIONAL TRIM TAB
REPLACED WITH FIXED
BALANCE TAB ON RUDDER

CANOPY DECK ACCESS
PANEL ADDED TO CANOPY

TAIL LIGHT MOVED TO
FAIRING ABOVE TAIL
PIPE

FUEL VENT ADDED
ON AFT FUSELAGE

DETAIL & SCALE, 1/72nd SCALE, COPYRIGHT © DRAWING BY LLOYD JONES

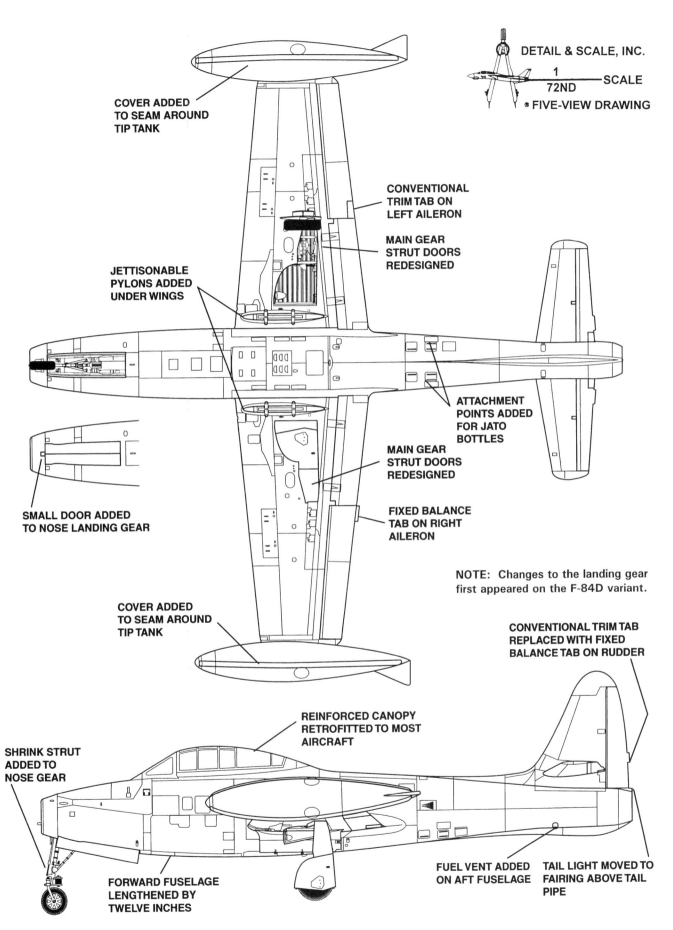

COVER ADDED
TO SEAM AROUND
TIP TANK

CONVENTIONAL
TRIM TAB ON
LEFT AILERON

MAIN GEAR
STRUT DOORS
REDESIGNED

JETTISONABLE
PYLONS ADDED
UNDER WINGS

DETAIL & SCALE, INC.

1
72ND — SCALE

® FIVE-VIEW DRAWING

ATTACHMENT
POINTS ADDED
FOR JATO
BOTTLES

MAIN GEAR
STRUT DOORS
REDESIGNED

FIXED BALANCE
TAB ON RIGHT
AILERON

SMALL DOOR ADDED
TO NOSE LANDING GEAR

NOTE: Changes to the landing gear
first appeared on the F-84D variant.

COVER ADDED
TO SEAM AROUND
TIP TANK

CONVENTIONAL TRIM TAB
REPLACED WITH FIXED
BALANCE TAB ON RUDDER

REINFORCED CANOPY
RETROFITTED TO MOST
AIRCRAFT

SHRINK STRUT
ADDED TO
NOSE GEAR

FORWARD FUSELAGE
LENGTHENED BY
TWELVE INCHES

FUEL VENT ADDED
ON AFT FUSELAGE

TAIL LIGHT MOVED TO
FAIRING ABOVE TAIL
PIPE

DETAIL & SCALE, 1/72nd SCALE, COPYRIGHT © DRAWING BY LLOYD JONES

F84E & F-84G EJECTION SEAT DETAILS

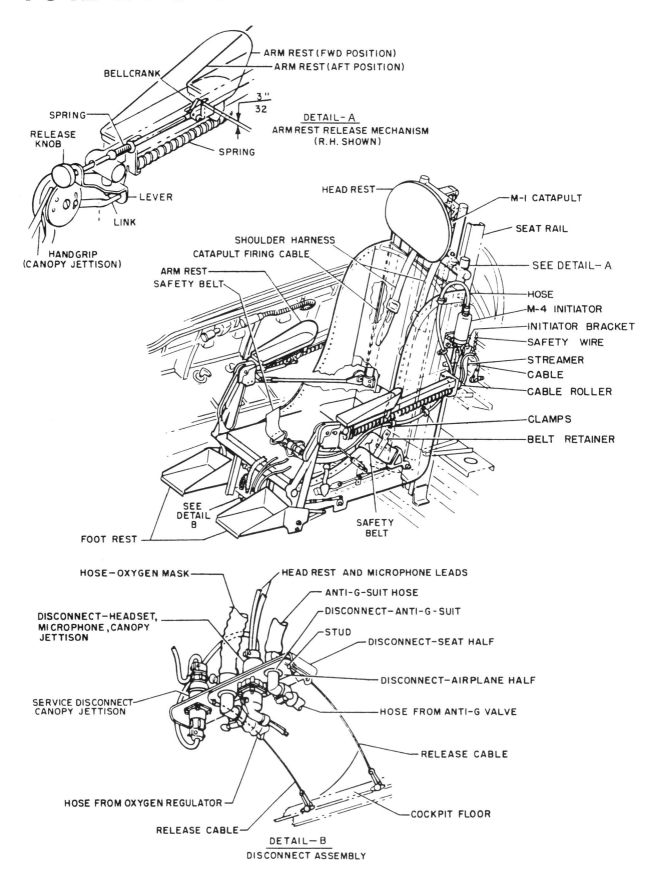

ARM REST (FWD POSITION)
ARM REST (AFT POSITION)
BELLCRANK
SPRING
RELEASE KNOB
$\frac{3"}{32}$
DETAIL-A
ARM REST RELEASE MECHANISM
(R.H. SHOWN)
SPRING
LEVER
LINK
HANDGRIP
(CANOPY JETTISON)

HEAD REST
M-I CATAPULT
SEAT RAIL
SEE DETAIL-A
SHOULDER HARNESS
CATAPULT FIRING CABLE
ARM REST
SAFETY BELT
HOSE
M-4 INITIATOR
INITIATOR BRACKET
SAFETY WIRE
STREAMER
CABLE
CABLE ROLLER
CLAMPS
BELT RETAINER
SEE DETAIL B
FOOT REST
SAFETY BELT

HOSE-OXYGEN MASK
HEAD REST AND MICROPHONE LEADS
ANTI-G-SUIT HOSE
DISCONNECT-ANTI-G-SUIT
DISCONNECT-HEADSET, MICROPHONE, CANOPY JETTISON
STUD
DISCONNECT-SEAT HALF
DISCONNECT-AIRPLANE HALF
SERVICE DISCONNECT CANOPY JETTISON
HOSE FROM ANTI-G VALVE
RELEASE CABLE
HOSE FROM OXYGEN REGULATOR
RELEASE CABLE
COCKPIT FLOOR
DETAIL-B
DISCONNECT ASSEMBLY

Features on the ejection seat used in the larger cockpits of the F-84E and F-84G are identified in this drawing from the erection and maintenance manual. For photographs of the ejection seat's details, see pages 42 and 43. (USAFM)

THUNDERJET COLORS

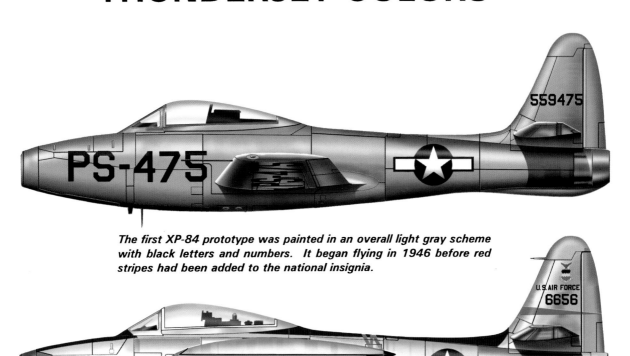

The first XP-84 prototype was painted in an overall light gray scheme with black letters and numbers. It began flying in 1946 before red stripes had been added to the national insignia.

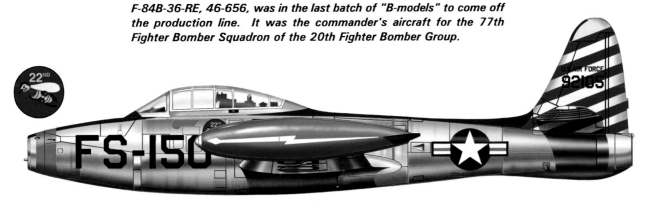

F-84B-36-RE, 46-656, was in the last batch of "B-models" to come off the production line. It was the commander's aircraft for the 77th Fighter Bomber Squadron of the 20th Fighter Bomber Group.

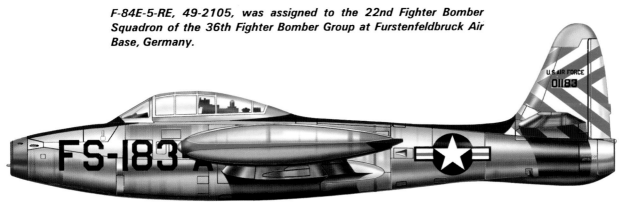

F-84E-5-RE, 49-2105, was assigned to the 22nd Fighter Bomber Squadron of the 36th Fighter Bomber Group at Furstenfeldbruck Air Base, Germany.

Red and white markings were used on Thunderjets assigned to the 9th Fighter Bomber Squadron of the 49th Fighter Bomber Wing. This F-84E-21-RE is shown as it appeared in June 1951.

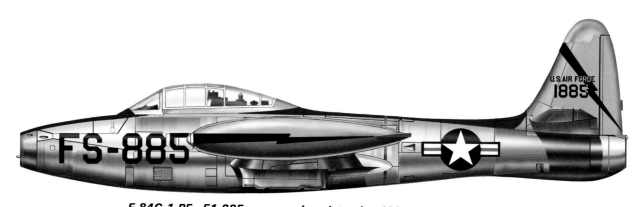

F-84G-1-RE, 51-885, was assigned to the 493rd Fighter Bomber Squadron of the 48th Fighter Bomber Group.

The 308th Fighter Bomber Squadron of the 31st Fighter Bomber Wing operated F-84G-1-RE, 51-821, in these yellow markings.

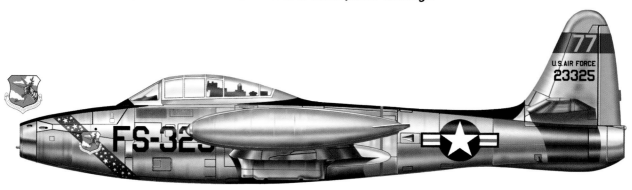

After the 31st was redesignated as a Fighter Escort Wing, the markings were changed to those shown here on F-84G-41-RE, 52-3325.

Denmark painted some of its Thunderjets in this gray and olive green camouflage scheme. F-84G-16-RE, 51-10600, was one of 2,236 F-84Gs supplied to foreign air forces under the Military Assistance Program.

F-84B COLORS

Above: P-84B, 45-59497, was the first production Thunderjet to be delivered to the U. S. Army Air Forces, and it was the only P-84B-2-RE built. It was later redesignated F-84B-2-RE, but then the designation was changed a second time to F-84B-4-RE.

(Col. R. Merritt via Menard)

Below: F-84B-26-RE, 46-586, was assigned to the 14th Fighter Group and had commander's stripes on the fuselage when this photograph was taken in September 1948. Note the mix of PS and FS prefixes in the buzz numbers soon after the pursuit designation was changed to fighter in June 1948. (W. Balogh via Menard)

F-84C COLORS

Above: F-84C-2-RE, 47-1447, has diagonal red stripes on its vertical tail and a red exhaust cone. It was assigned to the 58th Fighter Squadron of the 33rd Fighter Group.

(C. Graham via Menard)

Left and below: F-84C-11-RE, 47-1550, and F-84C-16-RE, 47-1587, were squadron commanders' aircraft within the 31st Fighter Group. Both photographs were taken during the 1948 time frame. Note the commander's stripes on the aft fuselage of each aircraft.

(Both E. Galbraith via Menard)

F-84D COLORS

Above: *F-84D-5-RE, 48-715, was assigned to the 79th Fighter Squadron of the 20th Fighter Group when this photograph was taken in 1949.*
(E. Galbraith via Menard)

Right: *Standard markings for the "Flying Yankees" of the Connecticut Air National Guard are painted on F-84D-1-RE, 48-647. Note that this aircraft has been retrofitted with the reinforced canopy.*
(P. Paulsen via Menard)

Below: The Connecticut ANG painted all upper surfaces on F-84D-5-RE, 48-721, with a bright orange color and used the aircraft as a target tug. The photograph is dated October 1954.
(P. Paulsen via Menard)

F-84E COLORS

Above: F-84E-5-RE, 49-2186, was assigned to the 23rd Fighter Bomber Squadron of the 36th Fighter Bomber Group based at Furstenfeldbruck Air Base, Germany. (Menard collection)

Left: These F-84Es were also assigned to the 23rd Fighter Bomber Squadron of the 36th Fighter Bomber Group. The photograph was taken during February 1952.

(F. Justice via Menard)

Below: The red and white markings on F-84E-5-RE, 49-2155, indicated that it was assigned to the 22nd Fighter Bomber Squadron of the 36th Fighter Bomber Group.

(Menard collection)

Above: These F-84Es were assigned to the 512th Fighter Bomber Squadron of the 406th Fighter Bomber Group. (LtCol. F. Smith via Menard)

Right: F-84E-1-RE, 49-2067, was redesignated EF-84E (the E prefix standing for "exempt"), and it was used as a test aircraft at Edwards Air Force Base. (Menard collection)

Below: F-84E-30-RE, 51-687, was assigned to the 9th Fighter Bomber Squadron of the 49th Fighter Bomber Wing. It had the name "SANDY" painted in yellow on the side of its fuselage. (E. Galbraith via Menard)

Above: F-84E-30-RE, 51-685, from the 158th Fighter Bomber Squadron of the 116th Fighter Bomber Wing, turns toward its target with two 500-pound bombs under its wings.
(R. McCormick via Menard)

Left: F-84Es of the 31st Fighter Escort Wing are prepared for gunnery practice in 1950. During the time they flew Thunderjets, the 31st was designated a fighter bomber wing, a fighter escort wing, and finally a strategic escort wing. (Menard collection)

Below: Late in their service life, these F-84Es were assigned to the Ohio Air National Guard at Springfield ANGB.
(Menard collection)

Above: F-84E-25-RE, 51-536, was flown by Lt. Donald James when he was assigned to the 8th Fighter Bomber Squadron of the 49th Fighter Bomber Wing in Korea. Note the red U. S. AIR FORCE painted across the yellow and black markings on the vertical tail.

(Col. D. James via Menard)

Right: Because James and his crew chief were both from Indiana, this Thunderjet was named "HOOSIER HOTSHOT," and this was lettered in yellow on the left side of the nose.   (Col. D. James via Menard)

The squadron insignia was painted on both sides of the nose next to the intake. The 8th Fighter Bomber Squadron was called the "Black Sheep."

(Col. D. James via Menard)

The yellow and black markings applied to the tip tanks are shown here. Also note the details of the navigation light on the front end of the tank.

(Col. D. James via Menard)

F-84E COCKPIT DETAILS & COLORS

F-84E-21-RE, 50-1143, is on display at the U. S. Air Force Museum in Dayton, Ohio, and its cockpit remains in very good condition. The photographs on this page and the next provide an excellent reference for the details and colors found in the cockpits of both F-84Es and F-84Gs. This close-up shows details of the gun sight and reflector glass.

Details on the instrument panel were standard when compared to those found in other early U. S. jet fighters of the late 1940s and early 1950s. Except for engine gages, most instruments were the same as the ones that had been used in U. S. propeller-driven fighters of World War II. Also note the auxiliary panel at the forward end of the right console.

The flat black control grip was covered with buttons and switches, and the control column was Interior Green. The basic cockpit and the floor were also painted Interior Green.

Most of the items on the right console were related to electrical systems and included lighting switches, controls for the Identification, Friend or Foe (IFF) system, and the radio control panel.

Circuit breakers and reset switches covered much of the left side of the cockpit. The red fuel selector control valve is visible on the edge of the console near the front of the seat.

Details of the throttle quadrant are illustrated here. Also note the auxiliary panel forward of the throttle quadrant. It has the landing gear control lever and lights to indicate that the gear is down and locked.

Above left and right: Features on the back of the ejections seat, the head rest, and the shoulder harness are visible in these two views. Note that the aircraft's serial number is painted on the seat back.

Right: Early U. S. ejection seats had a red ejection handle on the right side. To eject, the pilot would squeeze the two parts of the handle together. Also note the arm rest on the side of the seat. Each arm rest could be released and moved aft if desired.

Below: Colors of the items mounted aft of the seat are visible through the canopy in this photograph taken from the left side. A drawing identifying these items can be found on page 62.

F-84G COLORS

Above: F-84Gs in the 522nd Fighter Escort Squadron of the 27th Fighter Escort Wing were painted with red markings on the nose, tip tanks, and tail. (Col. D. Maggert via Menard)

Left: F-84Gs of the 31st Fighter Escort Wing were photographed at Hickam Air Base, Hawaii, during Fox Peter One. This was the first deployment of fighters across the Pacific using in-flight refueling.
(Bgen. N. Gaddis via Menard)

Below: F-84G-1-RE, 51-821, was assigned to the 308th Fighter Escort Squadron of the 31st Fighter Escort Wing. It has a full load of thirty-two rockets including six under each wing tip. (R. Williams via Menard)

Above: After transitioning to F-84Gs from F-84Es, the 8th Fighter Bomber Squadron of the 49th Fighter Bomber Wing changed its markings from those shown on page 41 to these markings on F-84G-26-RE, 51-11197. The buzz number has been moved from the nose to the aft fuselage, and U. S. AIR FORCE has been lettered on the nose in Insignia Blue. Also note the refueling probe installed in each of the tip tanks. (Menard collection)

Right: "No! Help Wanted" was an F-84G-16-RE assigned to the 310th Fighter Bomber Squadron of the 58th Fighter Bomber Wing in Korea.
(J. McCollum via Menard)

Training rockets and bombs are loaded on F-84G-1-RE, 51-821. Live rockets would have olive drab warheads with yellow bands and silver fuses on the tips.
(LtCol. J. Meierdierck via Menard)

This Thunderjet has live 1000-pound bombs loaded on the inboard wing pylons, while 100-pound bombs are attached to racks outboard of the landing gear. Also note the Chromate Yellow primer on the inside of the landing gear door. (E. Galbraith via Menard)

Above: Maintenance personnel work in the gun bay of F-84G-1-RE, 51-750. This Thunderjet was assigned to the 522nd Fighter Escort Squadron of the 27th Fighter Escort Group.
(Col. D. Maggert via Menard)

Left: These F-84Gs from the 27th Fighter Escort Wing were painted in very colorful markings for use in an official Air Force film on air tactics.
(L. Davis via Menard)

"New Orleans Kid" was an F-84G-10-RE assigned to the 111th Fighter Bomber Squadron of the 136th Fighter Bomber Group. (Lt. Col. T. Grassia via Menard)

F-84G-15-RE, 51-1225, was redesignated NF-84G and used in the ZELMAL tests. It was photographed at Bolling Air Force base in 1955. (Menard collection)

FOREIGN THUNDERJETS

Above: This F-84G was assigned to the Imperial Iranian Air Force, and it is painted in the standard markings used on Thunderjets operated by Iran.
(A. Gravatt via Menard)

Right: Far more elaborate markings have been applied to this Iranian F-84G which was used in Iran's aerobatic team. Much of the design appears to have been copied directly from markings used by the U. S. Air Force's "Thunderbirds" on their F-84Gs. (A. Gravatt via Menard)

Below: Colorful markings have been applied to this F-84G that was operated by the Thai Air Force. The markings are appealing without being overly elaborate. (Menard collection)

Above and left: Nationalist China was one of the nations that received F-84Gs under the Military Assistance Program. In fact, almost three times as many F-84Gs were produced for the air forces of foreign nations than were delivered to the U. S. Air Force.
(Above; Menard collection, left; Ochs via Menard)

Below: The Royal Danish Air Force operated Thunderjets into the 1960s, including F-84G-16-RE, 51-10720.
(G. Pennick via Menard)

F-84G

The F-84G was the definitive version of the Thunderjet series, and it established several important firsts in the history of fighter-bombers. F-84G-20-RE, 51-11245, has the later perforated speed brake beneath its fuselage.
(Williams via Jones)

Although its external appearance was essentially the same as the previous F-84E, the F-84G represented a considerable improvement in performance capabilities. The two most easily identifiable external differences were as a result of the change to the more powerful J35-A-29 powerplant which provided an additional 600 pounds of thrust over the J35-A-17 used in the F-84E. A blow-in door was located on each side of the forward fuselage to provide additional air to the engine when the aircraft was idling or taxiing slowly on the ground. The nozzle at the end of the tail pipe on the -29 engine was a little shorter than that on the -17, and its aft end was almost even with the trailing edge of the rudder. With the earlier engine, the nozzle had extended aft a few inches further than the edge of the rudder.

The F-84G was also the first Thunderjet variant to be produced with the reinforced canopy from the beginning, although this feature was retrofitted to all earlier versions remaining in service.

Close examination of the leading edge of the left wing would reveal a new set of panel lines near the root. These indicated the location of doors that covered the in-flight refueling receptacle that was used with the flying boom refueling system designed originally for long range bombers. With this feature, the F-84G became the first

production fighter-bomber equipped with a single-point in-flight refueling capability. As an alternative, probes could also be added to the front inboard side of each tip tank for use with the probe and drogue system.

Because of the long range capability that the in-flight refueling system permitted, the F-84G was also fitted with an autopilot to reduce pilot fatigue on flights of extended duration.

Another improvement was the addition of an A-4 gun sight which was added beginning with the eighty-sixth production F-84G. Later, this would be replaced with an APG-30 radar gun sight or a Mk 18. Starting with the 301st F-84G, a new instrument landing system was installed, and the ability to deliver nuclear weapons was added in late 1951, about six months after deliveries began. When this happened, the F-84G became the first fighter-bomber to have an atomic capability.

During the F-84G-10-RE production block, the design of the speed brake beneath the fuselage was changed. All previous Thunderjet variants had a speed brake with four rectangular slots. Beginning with F-84G-10-RE, 51-1079, a new speed brake with numerous circular perforations replaced the original design. Details of both speed brakes can be found in the drawings and photographs on page 66. It has been reported elsewhere that the later speed brake was retrofitted to earlier aircraft, but if this was done at all, the practice was very limited.

Deliveries of F-84Gs began in July 1951, and the following month, the 31st Fighter Escort Wing began to receive their F-84Gs at Turner Air Force Base, Georgia. The 27th Fighter Escort Wing at Bergstrom Air Force Base, Texas, followed soon thereafter as the Strategic

F-84G-1-RE, 51-964, is about to touch down on the runway at Wethersfield, England. This Thunderjet was assigned to the 79th Fighter Bomber Squadron of the 20th Fighter Bomber Wing. Note the placement of the buzz number on the aft fuselage behind the national insignia. (USAFM)

Air Command moved to equip its escort wings with fighters that could utilize the same flying boom method of in-flight refueling that its new jet bombers used.

By mid-1952, F-84Gs were deployed in strength to the Far East where they began flying combat missions in Korea. In the Far East, Air Force tankers were equipped only with the probe and drogue system for in-flight refueling, so probes were added to the tip tanks to make these F-84Gs compatable with the available tankers in that theater.

The capability of the F-84G using in-flight refueling was demonstrated when the 31st Fighter Escort Wing flew from Turner Air Force Base, Georgia, to Misawa Air Base in Japan in the summer of 1952. This deployment of fifty-eight Thunderjets, called Operation Fox Peter

One, dramatically confirmed the importance of the in-flight refueling capability and proved the concept of deploying fighters quickly to any point on the globe where they were needed. A few months later, in October 1952, the 27th Fighter Escort Wing flew from Bergstrom Air Force Base, Texas, to the Far East in Operation Fox Peter Two.

Because of its excellent flying qualities, the Thunderjet was also one of the first jets to be used by flight demonstration teams in the U. S. Air Force. In the United States Air Forces Europe (USAFE), the "Skyblazers," were formed as part of the 36th Fighter Bomber Group at Furstenfeldbruck Air Base, Germany. The team flew snows in Europe and Africa using F-84Es assigned to the group. During 1953, the team also borrowed F-84Gs from the 27th Fighter Escort Wing at Bergstrom Air Force Base, Texas, for a show in Detroit, Michigan. The fa-

Armed with rockets and bombs, the pilot of this F-84G is ready to taxi to the runway. The arrow markings are those of the 508th Strategic Fighter Wing.
(Williams via Jones)

F-84G-1-RE, 51-821, was assigned to the 308th Fighter Escort Squadron of the 31st Fighter Escort Wing. The markings on the nose, tip tanks, and tail were yellow.
(General W. D. Dunham via Taylor and the USAFM)

mous "Thunderbirds" also flew F-84Gs as their first aircraft after being formed as the official flight demonstration team for the U. S. Air Force in May 1953.

A total of 3,025 F-84Gs were produced, of which 789 were flown by the U. S. Air Force. The remaining 2,236 equipped the air forces of thirteen different nations. Within NATO, these included Belgium, Denmark, France, Greece, Italy, The Netherlands and Norway. Nationalist China, Iran, Thailand, Turkey, Yugoslavia, and Portugal also acquired F-84Gs under the Mutual Defense Assistance Program which was later renamed the Military Assistance Program in 1954.

DATA

Version	F-84G
Number Built	3,025
Powerplant	Allison J35-A-29
Static Thrust	5,600 pounds
Maximum Speed	622 mph
Cruising Speed	483 mph
Climb	9.4 minutes to 35,000 feet
Ceiling	40,750 feet
Range	2,000 miles*
Internal Fuel Capacity	452 gallons
Total Fuel Capacity	1,372 gallons
Empty Weight	11,095 pounds
Maximum Gross Take-off Weight	23,525 pounds

* Without in-flight refueling.

The 36th Fighter Bomber Group formed the "Skyblazers" flight demonstration team in Germany. Although this team was never officially recognized by the U. S. Air Force, it represented USAFE at numerous air shows, particularly in the European Theater. Usually the team flew F-84Es which were assigned to the 36th Fighter Bomber Group, but it borrowed F-84Gs from the 27th Fighter Escort Wing at Bergstrom Air Foce Base, Texas, for a show in Detroit, Michigan. F-84G-5-RE, 51-1065, was one of the borrowed Thunderjets that was painted in the "Skyblazers'" markings for that show. (USAFM)

The only officially recognized flight demonstration team in the U. S. Air Force is the "Thunderbirds" based at Nellis, Air Force Base, Nevada. When they were formed in 1953, the F-84G was chosen as the team's first aircraft because of its excellent flying qualities. The planes were painted in scalloped red, white, and blue markings very similar to those still used today on the team's F-16 Fighting Falcons. F-84G-26-RE, 51-16719, was one of the original aircraft assigned to the "Thunderbirds," and it is shown here as it appeared in 1953 with the team's original markings. (Williams via Jones)

Above: This F-84G is being fueled with fuming nitric acid for use with its experimental auxiliary rocket motor. The rocket motor was tested as an alternative to the standard JATO bottles as a way to get the Thunderjet airborne more quickly with heavy loads. (USAFM)

Left: At sea level, and on a 100-degree day, the YLR63-AJ-1 liquid rocket motor could get an F-84G weighing 23,200 pounds airborne with only a 3,500-foot ground roll. But the system proved impractical for operational use, and it did not replace standard JATO units. (USAFM)

Left: Several F-84Gs were used with project ZELMAL (Zero Length Launch and Mat Landing), conducted by the Glen L. Martin Company. The aircraft was launched using a rocket booster from a trailer like that used for Matador and Mace missiles, and it would return to land on an air-cushioned mat. Tests were also conducted using conventional landing gear. The purpose of the program was to develop a way in which fighters could be dispersed away from air bases to enhance survivability. The pneumatic landing mat provided a safe place to recover in the event runways had been destroyed or damaged beyond use during an attack. Although similar tests were conducted with a number of different aircraft types, the system was never deployed operationally. (USAFM)

F-84G DETAILS

The F-84G was the first fighter produced with provisions for the flying boom refueling system. The receptacle was covered by doors in the leading edge of the left wing near the root, and they have been opened to reveal the receptacle for the boom.

Although there were a few minor differences, the details in the cockpit of an F-84G were very similar to those in the F-84E. The colors would also be the same as for the F-84E as illustrated on pages 42 and 43. (USAFM)

Right: The Allison J35-A-29, as used in the F-84G, had 600 more pounds of thrust than the versions used in the previous F-84D and F-84E. An auxiliary blow-in door was added to each side of the forward fuselage to provide additional air to the engine when the aircraft was sitting still on the ramp or taxiing at slow speeds. This is the door on the right side.

F-84G, 1/72nd SCALE, FIVE-VIEW DRAWINGS

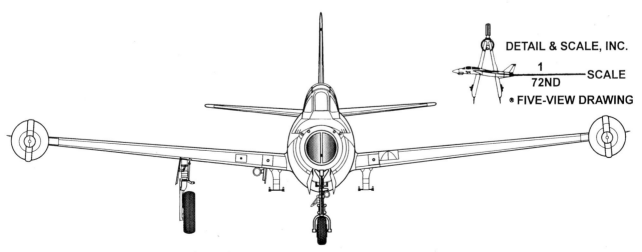

DETAIL & SCALE, INC.

$\dfrac{1}{72\text{ND}}$ SCALE

® FIVE-VIEW DRAWING

DETAIL & SCALE, 1/72nd SCALE, COPYRIGHT © DRAWING BY LLOYD JONES

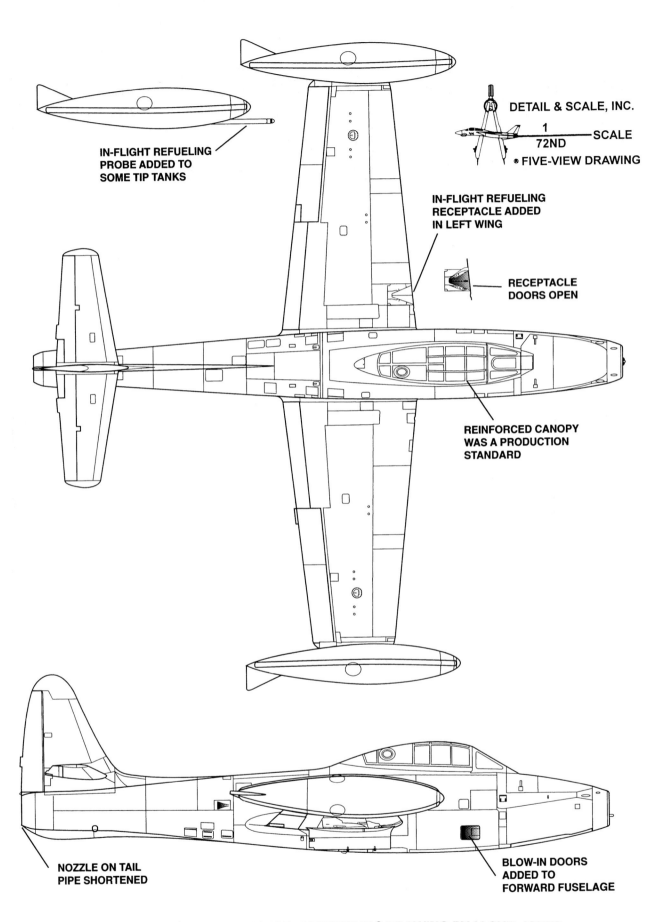

IN-FLIGHT REFUELING
PROBE ADDED TO
SOME TIP TANKS

DETAIL & SCALE, INC.

1
72ND — SCALE

® FIVE-VIEW DRAWING

IN-FLIGHT REFUELING
RECEPTACLE ADDED
IN LEFT WING

RECEPTACLE
DOORS OPEN

REINFORCED CANOPY
WAS A PRODUCTION
STANDARD

NOZZLE ON TAIL
PIPE SHORTENED

BLOW-IN DOORS
ADDED TO
FORWARD FUSELAGE

DETAIL & SCALE, 1/72nd SCALE, COPYRIGHT © DRAWING BY LLOYD JONES

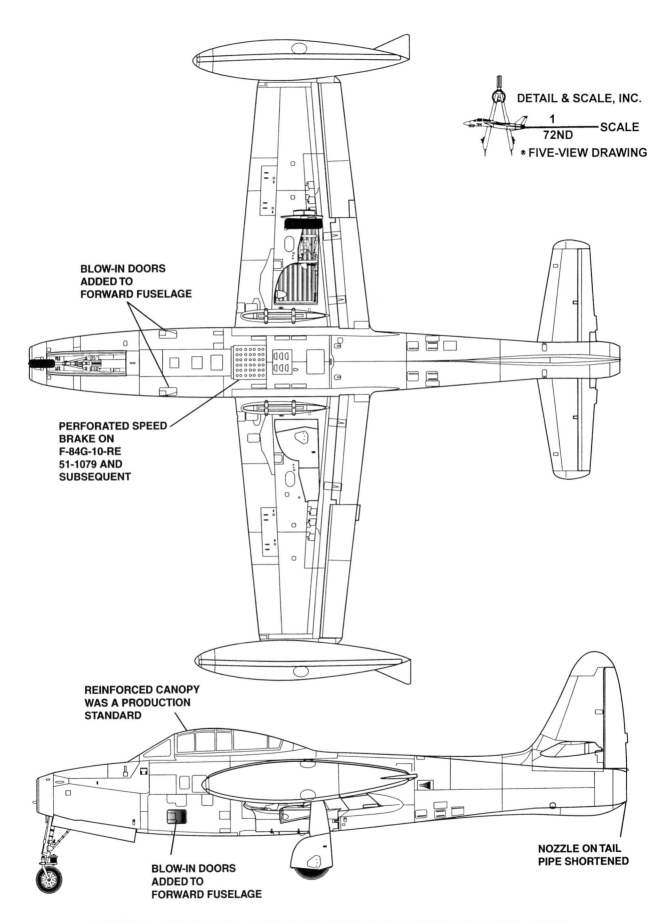

BLOW-IN DOORS
ADDED TO
FORWARD FUSELAGE

PERFORATED SPEED
BRAKE ON
F-84G-10-RE
51-1079 AND
SUBSEQUENT

DETAIL & SCALE, INC.

$\frac{1}{72ND}$ SCALE

® FIVE-VIEW DRAWING

REINFORCED CANOPY
WAS A PRODUCTION
STANDARD

NOZZLE ON TAIL
PIPE SHORTENED

BLOW-IN DOORS
ADDED TO
FORWARD FUSELAGE

DETAIL & SCALE, 1/72nd SCALE, COPYRIGHT © DRAWING BY LLOYD JONES

THUNDERJET DETAILS
LANDING GEAR DETAILS

1. AIR VALVE
2. SHRINK STRUT UNIVERSAL LINK
3. SHRINK STRUT FAIRING DOOR
4. DOOR ACTUATING PIN
5. NOSE GEAR SHOCK STRUT
6. SHRINK STRUT
7. TOW LUGS
8. DOWNLOCK AND WARNING SWITCH
9. UPLOCK HOOK
10. UPLOCK RELEASE CABLE
11. SPRING CARTRIDGE – UPLOCK
12. DRAG STRUT SUPPORT
13. ACTUATING CYLINDER SUPPORT
14. ACTUATING CYLINDER

15. DOWNLOCK CYLINDER
16. DRAG STRUT
17. ACTUATOR-NOSE GEAR DOORS
18. TAXI LIGHT
19. SHIMMY DAMP & CENTERING SPRING

20. UPLOCK LUG
21. TORQUE ARMS
22. STATIC GROUND
23. WHEEL NUT
24. RETAINER
25. WHEEL
26. AXLE NUT
27. COTTER PIN
28. AXLE
29. ADAPTER

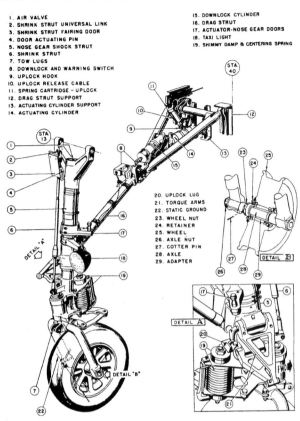

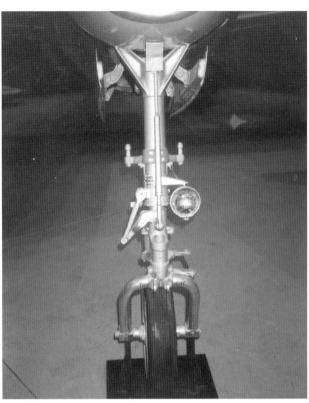

This drawing, taken from the erection and maintenance manual for the F-84G, illustrates and identifies the major components of the nose landing gear as used on the F-84E and F-84G. The photos on this page and the next five pages also illustrate the landing gear as used on these two versions of the Thunderjet. (USAFM)

A landing/taxi light was mounted on the left side of the nose landing gear strut. Also note the angle of the two nose gear doors when they are open.

The large shimmy dampener spring was located just above the tire on the back of the strut. Note the solid wheel on this aircraft.

The wheel on this aircraft is the earlier open spoke design. The shrink strut on the front of the main strut has a small fairing door at the top.

NOSE LANDING GEAR

The nose gear doors were not rectangular in shape. Instead, they were slightly tapered to the front, and there was a noticeable dip in the upper edge near the front.

An inside view of the right nose gear door reveals details including the two hinges. Note how the door hangs slightly away from the fuselage.

A close-up provides a good look at the aft hinge on the left nose gear door.

The actuating arm for the door was just aft of the forward hinge.

The forward end of the nose gear well and most of the drag strut can be seen in this view. Note the hydraulic cylinder and lines in the fork of the drag strut.

The wheel retracted into the aft end of the nose gear well. The well and the inside of the doors were usually painted with Chromate Yellow primer.

LEFT MAIN LANDING GEAR

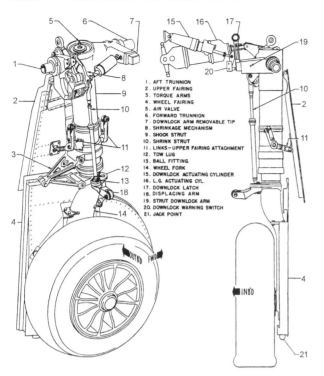

1. AFT TRUNNION
2. UPPER FAIRING
3. TORQUE ARMS
4. WHEEL FAIRING
5. AIR VALVE
6. FORWARD TRUNNION
7. DOWNLOCK ARM REMOVABLE TIP
8. SHRINKAGE MECHANISM
9. SHOCK STRUT
10. SHRINK STRUT
11. LINKS—UPPER FAIRING ATTACHMENT
12. TOW LUG
13. BALL FITTING
14. WHEEL FORK
15. DOWNLOCK ACTUATING CYLINDER
16. L.G. ACTUATING CYL.
17. DOWNLOCK LATCH
18. DISPLACING ARM
19. STRUT DOWNLOCK ARM
20. DOWNLOCK WARNING SWITCH
21. JACK POINT

Another drawing from the Thunderjet's erection and maintenance manual illustrates and identifies the major components of the left main landing gear.

A front view provides a good look at the angle of the strut to the wing as well as the correct angles of the two outer main gear doors when the gear is extended.

Details of the strut, wheel, and hydraulic lines are all visible here. Compare the details in this picture with the identified features in the drawing above.

An outside view shows how the two outer gear doors overlapped. Note how part of the USAF is painted on the gear doors.

Features inside the left main gear well are visible here. The inside of the well was usually painted with Chromate Yellow primer.

The hydraulic cylinder that extends and retracts the strut is visible in this close-up of the outer part of the left main gear well.

This view looks inward and aft into the inner part of the left main gear well. The inner door is in the closed position.

With the inner left main gear door open, the landing/taxi light is visible. Both of the inner gear doors had these lights.
(USAFM)

RIGHT MAIN LANDING GEAR

The shrink strut is visible in this rear view of the right main landing gear. Again, there is no hydraulic fluid in this aircraft, since it is preserved in a museum, so the oleo portion of the strut is collapsed.

A front view of the right main landing gear again shows the angle of the outer two doors. Note the small link that holds the upper door at the proper angle. The lower door is very close to the wheel and tire.

The lower of the two outer gear doors had a removeable panel to provide access for maintenance on the brake side of the wheel.

The inside of the lower gear door was usually painted with Chromate Yellow primer. The hydraulic brake lines were normally black.

An overall view looks up and outward into the right main landing gear well.

A close-up provides a look at the details where the strut joins the structure of the wing.

The part of the right main gear well where the wheel and tire fit when the gear is retracted can be seen here. The inner door is in the closed position.

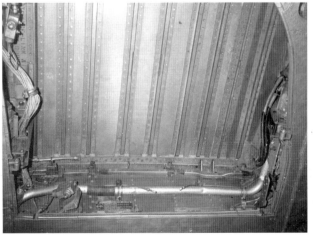

With the inner door removed, plumbing and other details at the inboard end of the well are visible. The interior of the well is painted with Chromate Yellow primer.

WINDSCREEN & CANOPY DETAILS

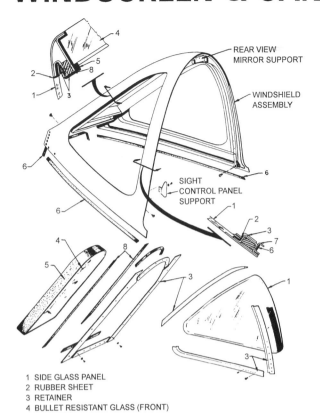

REAR VIEW
MIRROR SUPPORT

WINDSHIELD
ASSEMBLY

SIGHT
CONTROL PANEL
SUPPORT

1 SIDE GLASS PANEL
2 RUBBER SHEET
3 RETAINER
4 BULLET RESISTANT GLASS (FRONT)
5 EVERSEAL

COCKPIT PRESSURE REGULATOR
LOOP ANTENNA - AN/ARN-6 RADIO COMPASS
PULLEY - ELECTRICAL HARNESS
TOP FUSELAGE
LIGHT ASSEMBLY

SEAT
RAILS

FWD

NOTE:
CANOPY SHOWN
NEAR CLOSED POSITION

1 R. H. DISCONNECT - RADIO COMPASS
ANTENNA CABLES
2 ALIGNMENT-NOTCHES
3 L. H. DISCONNECT - RADIO COMMPAS
AND MISC CIRCUITS
4 LOCKWIRE
5 DISCONNECT - CANOPY CIRCUITS
6 ELECTRICAL HARNESS - CANOPY CIRCUITS
7 TAKE-UP SPRING

Above left: The components of the Thunderjet's windscreen are identified in this drawing from the erection and maintenance manual. **(USAFM)**

Above right: Another drawing identifies the items behind the seat that were mounted on a deck that moved with the canopy. **(USAFM)**

U.S. AIR FORCE F-84E-25-RE
A.F. SER NO. 51-604 A

NO STEP

Center left: The basic design of the F-84's windscreen was simple and quite strong.

Center right: From the side, the reflector glass of the gun sight can be seen beneath the front glass of the windscreen.

Left: The original canopy installed on Thunderjets was a simple sliding bubble design with no reinforcing strips. This design was initially used on all versions through the F-84E. **(USAFM)**

After structural problems were experienced with the original canopy, reinforcing strips were added on the F-84G production line. All earlier versions, including F-84Bs and F-84Cs in Air National Guard service, were retrofitted with these reinforced canopies.

Photographs indicate that there was more than one design used for the canopy framing. The items under the canopy were mounted on a deck that moved with the canopy itself.

Most reinforced canopies had a circular access panel on the right side. However, photographs indicate that this feature was not on all canopies.

The area immediately aft of the seat armor is visible here through the canopy. It was painted flat black.

An L-shaped panel line was at the aft end of the canopy frame.

FUSELAGE DETAILS

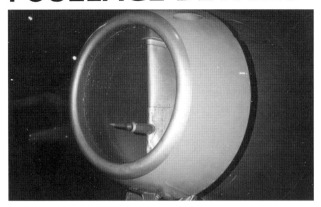

Beginning with the F-84D, the pitot probe was moved from the leading edge of the vertical tail to the splitter in the air intake. It remained in this location on the F-84E and F-84G.

On this page and the next, the markings and details on the fuselage of an F-84E are illustrated. They are basically the same for other Thunderjet variants. This is the forward fuselage on the left side.

Markings and details next to the cockpit on the left side are shown here. Red lettering inside a red rectangle warns that the aircraft is fitted with an ejection seat containing an explosive charge.

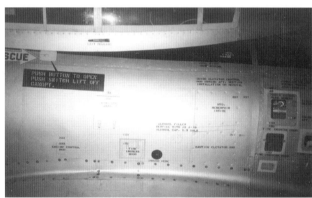

Emergency rescue markings are yellow and black. Yellow lettering on a black panel provides instructions about how to jettison the canopy so that the pilot can be rescued after a crash.

Black stencils cover the middle fuselage section. Yellow rectangles outline major access panels, and a red panel inside a yellow outline indicates the location of a fire ingress door.

Standard markings around the tail pipe are shown here, however these were not present on many aircraft. The item protruding from the aft fuselage is a fuel vent, and it is painted red.

These stencils are located just below the windscreen on the right side of the forward fuselage. Access panel numbers are painted on both the panels and the fuselage.

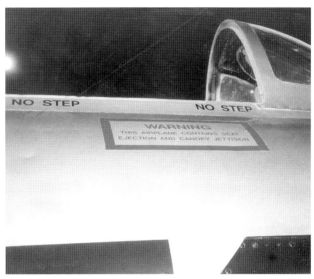

A red rectangle surrounds red stenciling warning that the aircraft is equipped with an ejection seat and an explosive device to jettison the canopy.

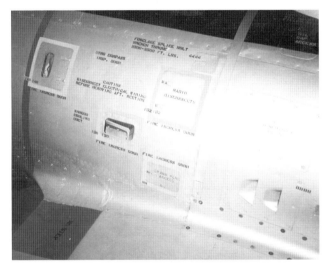

These marking are on the right side of the fuselage above the trailing edge of the wing. Again, yellow rectangles indicate the locations of important access panels.

These stencils indicate where the JATO unit is to be attached on the right side of the lower aft fuselage. The same markings are also on the left side.

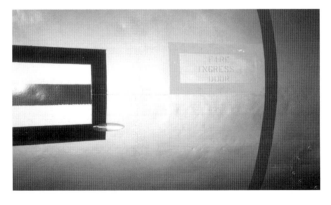

A fire ingress door was located on each side of the rear fuselage just aft of the red turbine warning stripe. The door was outlined in yellow, and in some cases, the area inside the yellow rectangle was painted red.

The blast warnings on the right side of the tail pipe area were the same as those on the left. A red fuel vent is also on this side of the aft fuselage.

SPEED BRAKE DETAILS

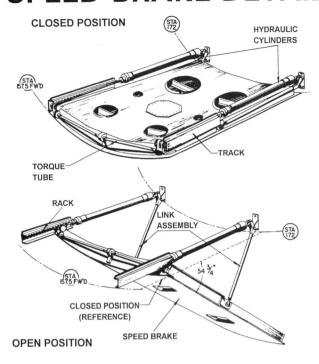

CLOSED POSITION

HYDRAULIC CYLINDERS

STA 172

STA 157.5 FWD

TORQUE TUBE

TRACK

RACK

LINK ASSEMBLY

STA 172

STA 157.5 FWD

54 3/4°

CLOSED POSITION (REFERENCE)

SPEED BRAKE

OPEN POSITION

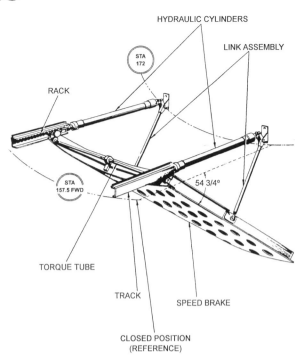

HYDRAULIC CYLINDERS

LINK ASSEMBLY

STA 172

RACK

STA 157.5 FWD

54 3/4°

TORQUE TUBE

TRACK

SPEED BRAKE

CLOSED POSITION (REFERENCE)

Two different speed brake designs were used on the F-84 Thunderjet. Most had this original design with four rectangular slots. **(USAFM)**

This perforated design was the second and later speed brake used. It was fitted on F-84G-10-RE, 51-1079, and all subsequent F-84Gs. **(USAFM)**

The speed brake could be opened to this angle to increase drag and slow the aircraft.

A front view of the original speed brake shows the four rectangular slots.

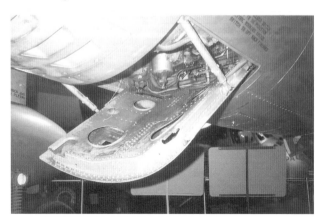

Details on the inside of the speed brake and inside the well are visible in this view from the right and slightly behind the brake.

F-84G-41-RE, 52-3271, has the later perforated speed brake. Its only difference from the earlier design was that numerous circular perforations replaced the four rectangular slots. **(USAFM)**

WING DETAILS

Each wing had a single gun mounted near the root. The barrel did not extend forward of the opening in the leading edge of the wing.

Spent shells and links were expended through slots just inboard of the landing gear. The inner landing gear door has been removed from this aircraft.

When the tip tanks were removed, the navigation light and connections for the tank were visible on the tip of the wing. Although it was fairly common to see F-84Bs and F-84Cs fly without their tanks, later versions of the Thunderjet almost always had them in place.

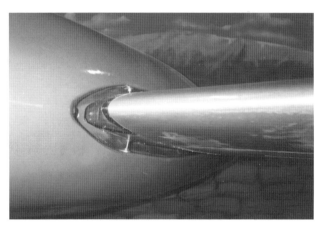

When the tank was installed, the navigation light fit into the slot in the tip tank. Note the anti-sway braces between the wing and the tank. A flexible seal would be added all the way around the tank and the wing before the aircraft could be flown, but it is not present here.

The trailing edge of the wing had standard flaps and ailerons. The point where the left flap meets the left aileron is shown here, and the trim tab is visible on the aileron.

The flap met the wing root in a stepped configuration. The lower half extended inboard further than the top forming an overlapping joint between the flap and the fairing on the fuselage.

Arming wires for the fuses on the rockets were attached into these two pair of slots on the underside of the wing.

A refueling filler point was located on top of each wing. This is the one on top of the left wing, and its location can be determined within the national insignia.

An underside view of the left flap shows the two large hinges. The flap is slightly extended, and the hinges and their covers are exposed. Also note the moveable trim tab on the left aileron.

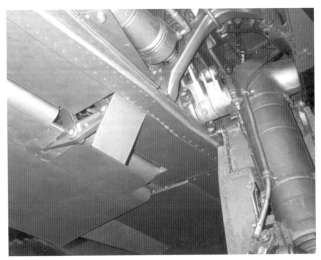

Thunderjets up through the F-84D had trim tabs on the rudder, elevators, and both ailerons. On the F-84E and F-84G, the trim tabs were on the left aileron and elevators only. This is the trim tab on the left aileron as seen from above.

Each of the flaps were mounted on two large hinges. As the flaps were extended, the hinges were exposed, and a small cover opened as shown here. This is the outer flap hinge on the left flap.

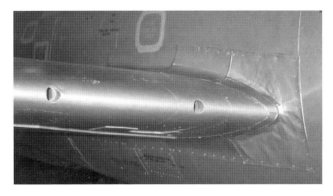

The port for the gun camera was located outboard of the wing gun on the leading edge of the right wing.

On the F-84E and F-84G, there was no moveable trim tab on the right aileron as there had been on the earlier versions of the Thunderjet. Instead, there was only a fixed balance tab.

Access to the wing guns was gained through panels on top of the wings. This is the panel on top of the right wing.

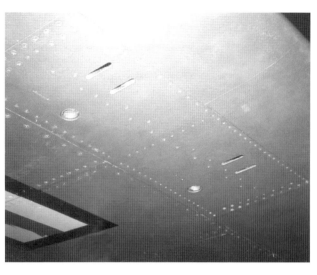

The slots for the rocket arming wires were outboard of the landing gear near the leading edge of the wing.

An underside view shows the partially extended right flap and the fixed tab on the aileron.

TIP TANK DETAILS

Tip tanks first appeared on the F-84B. The original tanks did not have a fin at the aft end, and there was no covering panel on the seam around the top and bottom of the tank.

Fuel could be vented from the aft end of each tank to lighten the aircraft for landing. The tanks were interchangeable, but this tank is mounted on the left wing of the aircraft.

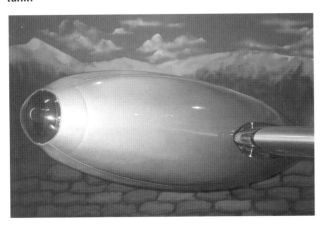

A clear dome was at the front of the tip tank, and it had the navigation light inside. The inboard half of the dome was usually painted a solid color to keep the light from flashing into the pilot's eyes.

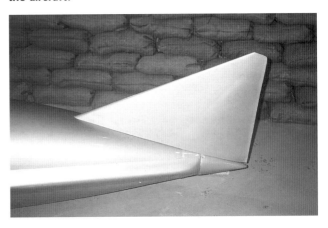

Beginning with the F-84D, fins were added to the rear of each tank on the outer edge. These were retrofitted to earlier aircraft, and they remained standard on all subsequent variants.

An underside view of the left wing shows how the tank mounted to the wing tip. The main mounts were in the wing tip, and small anti-sway braces were located in the slot between the tank and the wing tip.

A flexible seal was added between the wing tip and the tank to smooth airflow. The cover over the seam around the top and bottom of the tank is also visible on this photograph.

PYLON DETAILS

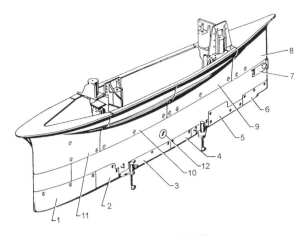

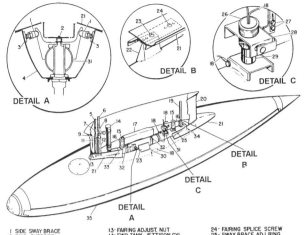

Above left: A drawing from the erection and maintenance manual identifies the details of the wing pylon as used on the F-84E and F-84G. (USAFM)

Above right: Features of the pylon and tank installation as used on the F-84E and F-84G are illustrated in this drawing from the manual. (USAFM)

Right: The pylons used on the F-84E and F-84G could be jettisoned, while on earlier variants, the pylons were fixed bomb racks. Note the considerable amount of stenciling on the pylon.

The two anti-sway braces are visible from this low angle.

A rear view of the pylon shows the marking on the small fairing at the aft end. This fairing was removed when small 100-pound practice bombs were loaded. The cocking cable fitted into the small slot on the trailing edge.

ROCKET ARMAMENT

ROCKET LOADING DETAILS

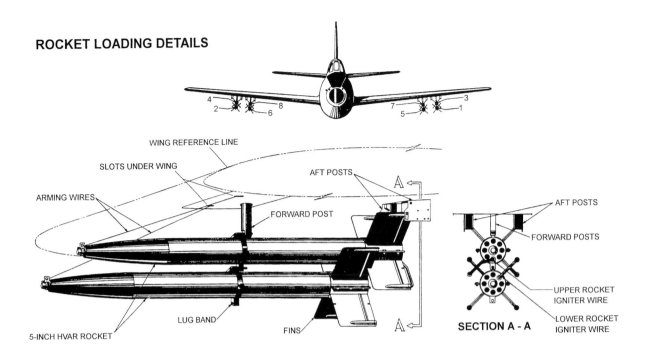

This drawing from the pilot's manual explains how rockets were loaded under the wings outboard of the landing gear. Notice how the arming wires extended between the fuses on the rockets and the slots in the underside of the wing. *(USAFM)*

Above: Armorers load rockets under the wings of an F-84E. *(USAFM)*

Right: A close-up provides a better look at 5-inch rockets loaded under the left wing. Note the aft posts near the upper fins of the top rockets. JATO units can be seen mounted under the fuselage in the background. *(USAFM)*

ROCKET LOADING AND FIRING SEQUENCE

ROCKETS ARE LOADED
IN REVERSE SEQUENCE
TO FIRING ORDER.

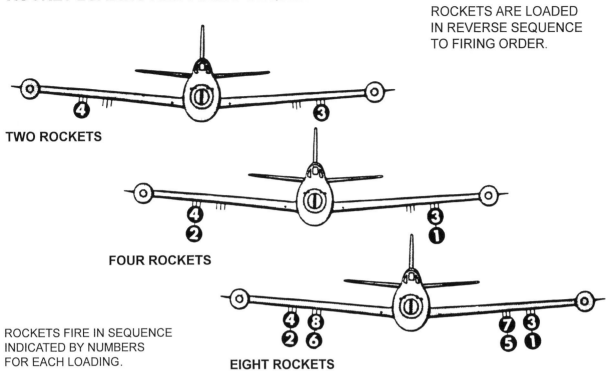

TWO ROCKETS

FOUR ROCKETS

ROCKETS FIRE IN SEQUENCE
INDICATED BY NUMBERS
FOR EACH LOADING.

EIGHT ROCKETS

Above: The rocket loading and firing sequence is illustrated in this drawing from the Thunderjet's pilot's manual. *(USAFM)*

Below: This F-84E has 5-inch rockets loaded in triples under its wings, while large 12-inch Tiny Tim rockets are mounted on the pylons. *(USAFM)*

TAIL DETAILS
VERTICAL TAIL DETAILS

The basic design of the Thunderjet's tail section did not change throughout production of all variants, but there were detail differences.

The F-84B and F-84C had a pitot probe on the leading edge of the vertical tail near the top. Beginning with the F-84D, the probe was moved to the splitter inside the engine inlet.

The XP-84 through the F-84D had a moveable trim tab at the base of the rudder.

The F-84E and F-84G did not have a moveable trim tab on the rudder, but there was a fixed balance tab on the trailing edge. This fixed balance tab was also fitted on some earlier versions with the trim tab as well.

HORIZONTAL TAIL DETAILS

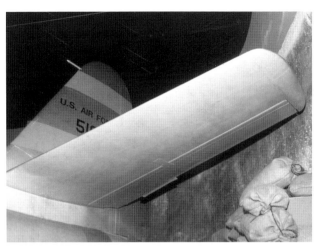

Thunderjets were fitted with conventional horizontal tail assemblies which included horizontal stabilizers and moveable elevators that extended from the vertical tail out to the tip cap.

Both elevators had moveable trim tabs and fixed balance tabs. The long balance tab is visible in this underside view of the left horizontal tail.

Each horizontal tail had a small access panel on top near the middle. What appears to be a hinge cover between the horizontal stabilizer and the elevator is actually a plate to hold the elevator in the neutral position on this aircraft that is now preserved in the Museum of Aviation at Warner Robins, Georgia.

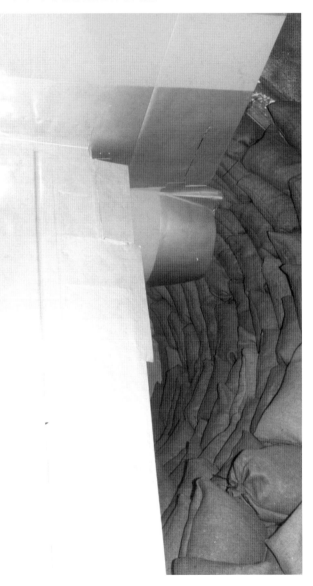

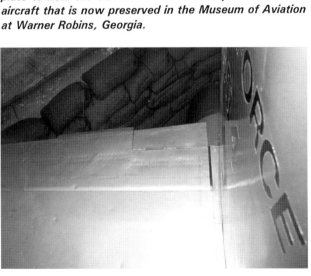

The moveable trim tab was located at the inboard end of the elevator. The fixed balance tab was just outboard of the trim tab. This is the top of the right elevator.

The fixed balance tab and moveable trim tab on the trailing edge of the left elevator are both visible in this view. These tabs were on all versions of the Thunderjet.

ENGINE DETAILS

The intake cone on the Allison J35 engine angled down at the front.

Accessories were located all around the forward end of the engine. This is the right front side.

Center left: The combustion chambers were located around the mid-section of the engine between the accessories and the tail pipe.

Center right: Only a few lines of plumbing surrounded the insulation blanket around the tail pipe.

Left: The exhaust nozzle on the tail pipe was actually part of the engine rather than the fuselage. The Allison J35 was a non-afterburning, axial-flow turbojet engine.

Details of the flame holder are visible in this photograph taken up inside the tail pipe. The nozzle at the end of the tail pipe was fixed, and it did not have the movable convergent/divergent nozzle or "eyelid" common on today's powerful afterburning engines.

The exhaust nozzle on the J35-A-17, used in the F-84E, was slightly longer than that on the J35-A-29 used in the F-84G. As a result, it extended a few inches past the trailing edge of the rudder, while the nozzle on the F-84G was almost even with the rudder's edge.

Center left: Details around the insulation blanket and the tail pipe on the left side of the engine are visible in this view.

Center right: The combustion chambers extended all the way around the center section of the engine.

Right: Numerous accessories also covered the front left side of the engine.

MODELERS SUMMARY

Note: Beginning with this volume, the usual Modelers Section is being reduced to a Modelers Summary. The summary will cover injection-molded plastic model kits of the subject aircraft from 1/144th scale through 1/32nd scale. Highlights of the better kits in each scale will be discussed, and recommendations will be made with respect to which kit or kits in each scale are the best for the serious scale modeler. The purpose of these recommendations is to help the modeler choose the best kit to use in each scale. Once a kit has been purchased, the modeler should compare the various features of the kit to the drawings and photographs in the book to determine how accurately specific details are represented. He can then decide what, if any, correcting or detailing work he wants to do to enhance the appearance of the model.

The best Thunderjet model in 1/72nd scale is from Heller. AeroMaster has also released an upgraded version of this kit with additional detailing parts. This Heller model was built by Stan Parker to represent an F-84G from the 77th Fighter Bomber Squadron of the 20th Fighter Bomber Group. **(Parker)**

GENERAL

The F-84 Thunderjet was an important early jet aircraft in the inventory of the United States Air Force as well as more than a dozen foreign nations, and it played a major role in the Korean War. The F-84G was the first production fighter to have in-flight refueling capability using the flying boom system, and it was the first fighter-bomber capable of delivering an atomic weapon. Both of these factors are very important "firsts" in military aviation. Therefore, it is surprising that so few scale models of the Thunderjet have been released during the fifty-plus years since it first flew. There are no kits of the Thunderjet in 1/144th scale or 1/32nd scale. Our comments below are therefore limited to 1/72nd and 1/48th scale kits.

1/72nd SCALE KITS

In 1/72nd scale, the clear choice is the Heller F-84G which has been on the market for approximately twenty years. While the kit is not up to today's standards, it is clearly better than the Plastyk/Inplast or Frog kits, and with some detailing work, it can be completed as an accurate representation of the F-84G. Panel lines are raised, there is no balance tab on the rudder, and the blow-in doors on the forward fuselage are too pronounced. The landing gear is not particularly well done, and most noticeably, the shrink strut is missing from the nose gear. Surprisingly, the tiny door at the top of the shrink strut is represented. The cockpit consists of a basic tub with consoles, and only an instrument panel, control column, seat, and gun sight are provided as detailing parts. Both speed brake designs are included, and there is a splitter to go in the inlet to prevent a hollow look inside the nose. Two external fuel tanks are provided to go on the pylons under the wings, and most shapes and outlines are correct.

To solve the detailing problems with the Heller kit, AeroMaster released an enhanced version with resin, etched metal, and vacu-formed parts as well as special edition decals. The detailing parts replace or enhance the cockpit, landing gear, wheel wells, and control surfaces. This special edition kit by AeroMaster solves all the detailing problems in the Heller kit except for the surface

scribing. It is well worth the extra price for someone who wants the model detailed to today's standards.

Another 1/72nd scale F-84G has been released under the Plastyk and Inplast labels. Regardless of issue, the kit is the same except for decals, and it is quite crude. While it shares some commonality with the Heller kit, it is not a direct copy, nor is it as well executed. Smaller parts, particularly the landing gear, are overly simplified and poorly molded. It is devoid of any surface detailing other than engraved control surfaces and a few major details. There is not even a representation of the doors for the refueling receptacle in the left wing root. The blow-in doors are simply depressions in the sides of the forward fuselage. Detailing is lacking throughout, and what little that is provided is often inaccurate or poorly represented. The outline of the fuselage is incorrect, and the cover around the seams on the fuel tanks are twice as big as they should be. Clear parts are provided for the canopy, windscreen, and the navigation lights at the forward end of each tip tank. All clear parts have a yellow tint, and the canopy and windscreen are too thick. Simply stated, we cannot recommend this kit.

Frog also had a 1/72nd scale Thunderjet many years ago. It had no cockpit, no wheel wells, and was simply a basic shape as were many early plastic models from the 1950s. It now has value only to collectors.

1/48th SCALE KITS

The first Thunderjet model to be issued in 1/48th scale was the Hawk F-84G which dates back to the 1950s. Like many early plastic models of jets, you could look in the inlet and see out the exhaust. The pilot's shoulders and head were molded on a shelf at the top of the fuselage, and there was no detailing. The smaller parts were very crude and usually oversized. The canopy did not have the reinforcing strips, and with all these shortcomings, the kit simply could not be completed as an accurate scale model of the Thunderjet.

It wasn't until the mid-1990s that modelers had a good F-84G in 1/48th scale with which to work. The French company, Battle Axe, issued a limited run kit with plastic, white metal, vacu-formed, etched metal, and resin parts. The basic assembly was made up of heavy plastic parts with recessed panel lines. However, a number of noticeable features like the refueling filler caps on top of the wings were missing, and other access panels and details were inaccurately represented. Balance tabs were missing from the rudder, elevators, and the right aileron, while the left aileron had the trim tab scribed in the top but not the bottom. A large resin part included the cockpit tub, nose gear well, splitter for the inlet, and a well for the speed brake. Other resin parts were provided for the interior of the main gear wells, wheels, tail pipe, seat, and canopy deck. The landing gear struts, anti-sway braces for the pylons, and some cockpit details were provided as white metal parts. Other cockpit details, navigation lights, a vent panel, door hinges, and both types of speed brakes were among the etched metal detailing parts. Two canopies and two sets of clear domes for the navigation lights at the front of the tip tanks were provided as vacu-formed parts. Now that the Tamiya Thunderjet is available, and the ProModeler kit will soon be released, this Battle Axe kit is more of a collector's item than a model to be built.

In 1998, Tamiya issued an excellent 1/48th scale F-84G kit. It is up to today's state of the art for plastic models with engraved panel lines, excellent detailing, and superb fit. Only a little filling and sanding is required around the nose ring at the inlet. Otherwise the kit fits together beautifully. We do recommend adding some plastic card behind the blow-in doors to prevent a "see-through" effect in the forward fuselage.

There are a number of enhancing parts to include a boarding ladder, a gun bay in the nose that can be opened to show a detailed interior, bombs or external tanks to go on the wing pylons, and JATO bottles for the underside of the aft fuselage. Contrary to some reviews that have been published about this kit, the JATO bottles are not shown backwards on the instruction sheet. The small nozzle on each unit should go to the rear as the instructions show it. Wing tips are provided if the tip tanks are to be left off, and the flaps can be assembled in the extended or retracted position.

Missing items that should have been provided include the 5-inch rockets to go under the wings, and the in-flight refueling probes for the tip tanks. All F-84Gs assigned to the Far East Air Force had both in-flight refueling systems, and markings for two of the F-84Gs on the decal sheet are for these aircraft.

Several modelers have expressed complaints about the fact that the wing pylons are molded as part of the underside of the wings. This does limit the modeler's options, and we agree that the complaints are justified. Another negative is that only the later style speed brake is included, so this again limits the aircraft than can be modeled. Only F-84Gs including serial number 51-1097 and subsequent had this later style speed brake with the round perforations. It would have been nice if Tamiya

Stan Parker used the excellent Tamiya F-84G kit to build this model of a Thunderjet from the 8th Fighter Bomber Squadron of the 49th Fighter Bomber Group. (Parker)

had added one additional part to represent the earlier style speed brake. The addition of this one part would have meant that any F-84G could be built from the kit.

The worst negative in the kit is the decal sheet. The decals are thick, and it is sometimes difficult to get the larger ones to conform tightly to surfaces. This is particularly true of the decals that go on the vertical tail. An interesting flaw concerns the information under the data plates. Magnifying the stenciling reveals that it is part of the history of the F-84G's development taken from a manual. It is not accurate stencilling information for any Thunderjet, so cut it away from the data plate you are using. The instrument panel decal is also very poor, and we would recommend taking time to paint the panel instead. Some of the badges and other artwork in the decals have inaccuracies, so we recommend using an after-market decal sheet.

Overall, this is an excellent kit. The only serious negatives are the substandard decal sheet and the limited options as to which F-84Gs can be modeled using the kit parts. Fit, detailing, and accuracy are quite good, and we recommend this kit.

In 1997, Revell-Monogram announced that it would release an F-84G in its ProModeler line of kits. The author did much of the research for the kit, and Bill Koster did the design work. Although the kit has been delayed until a release in 1999, the work on it done by the author during its development permits a brief preview of it here.

Both types of speed brakes will be provided in a set of etched metal parts so that any F-84G can be built. The etched metal parts also include an access ladder and buckles for the lap belt and shoulder harness. External ordnance will be quite extensive, and will include fuel tanks, 500-pound bombs, stacked 5-inch rockets, and even a tactical atomic weapon. The kit also will have both the refueling receptacle to go in the leading edge of the left wing and the refueling probes in the tip tanks.

Bill Koster has always done excellent design work as exemplified by the ProModeler SB2C-4 Helldiver. Although it is unfortunate that this Thunderjet model was delayed, it promises to be a kit of equal quality to the Helldiver. It will provide options not available in the Tamiya kit and will cost considerably less.

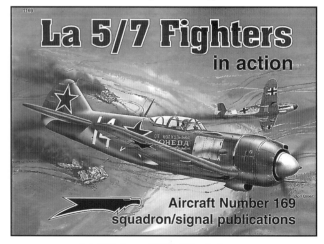